NOW
IS
THE TIME
TO
BELIEVE

THOMAS E. WALKER

Now Is the Time to Believe

The content of this book is based on a testimony of God's love and faith.

Published by Walkus Consulting Solutions and Reflections of Grace Outreach Ministries

Inspirational poems written by Denise P. Ford of Naima's Inspirational Melodies © (with permission)

ISBN: 978-0-9830162-2-9

Acknowledgments

I give honor to God and His Son, Jesus Christ, who have ordained and called me to speak on the goodness and matchless outpouring of grace and mercy that have been given to me and the world today. I thank the Holy Spirit, who has instructed me, in discernment, to compile the research and message of hope and love while writing this book. I offer this book as a writing of soul care and grace to bear witness of the unmerited favor that the Lord has shown me through my years. The Bible taught me to "Give Thanks unto the lord in all things for He is worthy and His mercy endures through all generations" (Psalm 107: 1 NKJV). This is my personal thank you to the Holy Trinity (God the Father, God the Son, and God the Holy Spirit) for giving me life, saving my life, and teaching me how to live a life that is pleasing to God.

I want to thank everyone who supported and prayed with me while writing this message of love. I especially want to thank my mentors and other spiritual leaders, Pastor Sam Estell (St. Louis), Pastor Robert L. Johnson, Jr. (Villa Park), Rev. James Bryant, and Celora Beeler (Detroit), who inspired me to move forward for the Lord and not look back when others stopped caring and sharing; bless you, you were there. A heartfelt thank you to my wife, Denise P. Ford-Walker, who listened, prayed, and stood with me by faith and love to pull me through my struggling times when they were harder than I realized; I love you so much. A special note: I want to bless and thank my mother, Elaine Brown, for giving me life and loving me unconditionally. I thank you, Mom, for encouraging me and blessing me as I move forth in my spiritual calling as teacher, pastor, and encourager. It means a lot to me to have your blessing and to hear you always tell me, "I'm proud of you" and "I love you"; I love you back, always.

I believe, I understand, and I know that they who endure to the end will receive a blessed reward.

Foreword

"It is admirably and *unapologetically* apologetic.

It is Theologically Sound.

This work is a post modern clarion call to its generation.

Elder Thomas E. Walker's work is both practical and applicable.

Encapsulated in this work is an exhaustive and engaging personal statement of faith, which every believer should document for their legacy's sake/posterity.

Walker understands and articulates the state of "the Leper" and how that spiritual condition has transcended the times and manifested itself in various forms. He also offers practical solutions to the end of this phenomena and the saving of this generation, no matter their station in life.

Retired, United States Army Cold War Veteran, Minister of The Gospel, Student of Life and God's Word are just a couple of titles that define this Propagator and Practitioner of the Gospel. Yet Elder Walker has lived on many levels, and through his experiences, herein contained, he's able to identify with anyone who comes in contact with this Gospel message. This book is not only readable, but it's also relatable.

This work possesses the experiences of a life traveler who has gone from just merely living life naturally to eternal life. Elder Walker takes you into the process of "winning Christ." Furthermore, he works out the process and walks you through the honesty and transparencies of what the Gospels and The Epistles are meant to convey for this postmodern generation.

It is a challenge to those in leadership to cite and correct authority abuse. It is also reminds them of their responsibility and duty, per scripture, to interpret scripture properly and train and teach the next generation. Simply stated, it is one's ministerial mantra to demystify and uncomplicate Christianity.

Upon completion of this book, the believer will be reinvigorated to righteous ascents, and for those who have not given themselves to Christ and have experienced so great a salvation, it will propel them to an inspired, exclaimed, and agreeable action that asserts, "Yes, now is the time to believe!"

—Dr. Marcel Townsel, D. Min.

Contents

GRACE

FINAL THOUGHTS

Introduction

"Many *are* the afflictions of the righteous, But the Lord delivers him out of them all." (Psalm 34:19; NKJV)

Now is the time for us to individually search and examine our hearts and ask, "Is God pleased with me and my life right now?" or "Have I truly made an effort to believe in God and what the Bible says about eternal life?" What do you believe? Can you be open to give God a chance to come into your life and show you what He can do?

Believing in God personally means that you are willing to live, learn, and love God's way. Serving God is a voluntary endeavor that every person who learns can follow. Now is the time to believe that God is Omnipresent, Omnipotent, and, more importantly, loving. We must believe that God is offering every person on this earth an opportunity of reconciliation through the blood sacrifice of His Son, Jesus Christ.

Our devoted belief in God's love and Jesus' ultimate love and sacrifice has to be freely given back to God as an answer to the question, "Have you received spiritual reconciliation back to God since you believed that He loves everyone so greatly and has a tremendous plan of eternal love, peace, grace, and purpose for each of us?"

Now is the time to believe that there is a *triune* voice reaching out to us through the pages of the Holy Bible, letting us know that God Loves, Jesus Saves, and the Holy Spirit Guides us, Comforts us, and Keeps us connected to the message of salvation and hope. The understanding of the word *triune,* means, one God working in three individuals known as, God the Father, God the Son, and God the Holy Spirit; performing three specific duties in our lives. There's a passage that I would like to leave with you to tell yourselves in the time of storms and turmoil, and it reads, "Even when I walk through the darkest valley, I will not be afraid, for you are close beside me. Your rod and your staff protect and comfort me … Surely your goodness and unfailing love will pursue me all the days of my life, and I will live in the house of the Lord forever" (Psalm 23:4, 6; NLT).

Now is the time to believe that we are never alone. We must believe that the power of the *triune* is constantly working in our lives to bring us to the most important moment of our lives; and that moment is the acceptance of salvation. Salvation and deliverance is offered by God through Christ by grace through faith. Deliverance means that we will allow the burden of pride and self-will to be lifted from our hearts so that we can completely leave our current situations or obstacles at the feet of Jesus Christ and trust that He can handle anything that comes our way. Believing and trusting in God is all about having faith in knowing that He is near and waiting for you to trust Him with your life. Today, I challenge you to believe that "there is nothing too hard for God."Jeremiah 32:27 NKJV

We must allow God's acceptance and Christ loving, compassion to rule our hearts so that the redemptive embodiment of Christ reveals that only what we do for Him will forever remain "good." Again, this can only come by understanding that we are at a time in our lives when we must believe that God loves us regardless of our situation. If we start building a prayer life that seeks help and peace through repentance and commitment, then God will reveal Himself with authority in each of our lives.

Our way of life should have attributes of being free from the entanglements of sin. We have to be willing to relinquish the inherent nature of sin and give it all up without question for God. God's grace and mercy are extended to all individuals who truly want and need Him to be Lord over their lives. So beloved, you no longer have to live a life that displeases God. You no longer need to accept your inherited sinful thoughts to be the only thoughts that lead and guide you from day to day; you can change your thoughts to reflect the will of God. God cares for us and loves us so much! That's why God has provided us with a way to be reconciled back to Him; and that way is Jesus. In the Bible, there's a verse of scripture called John 3:16 NKJV that affirms this as it tells us "For God so loved the world that He gave His only begotten Son, that whoever believes in Him should not perish but have everlasting life."

Additionally, in the Bible it tells us that God created us with freewill and the choice to voluntarily believe and worship Him; because our worship should be heartfelt and not a forced worship out of obligation or service to our Creator. In Proverbs 16:9 NKJV we learn this truthful wisdom that "A man's heart plans his way, but the Lord directs his steps." You must understand that God's will for mankind is to be redeemed and free from the devices of disobedience. However, disobedient curiosity and freewill caused mankind to choose the wrong path; as a result, we became self-centered, evolving creations that grew weaker and wiser to spiritual thoughts that were against the true purpose of worship to our Creator. This is called sin. Our genetic makeup was made in the image of God (our Creator), and we were made perfect in His spiritual characteristics of love, peace, and dominion; but our misguided freewill from an opposing force to God's plan drove us further and further from the purpose of worship and peace.

God will give us peace and joy that surpasses all of our understanding because He loves our freewill worship toward Him. Living a life that is pleasing to God has to be the primary reason why we accept Christianity as the true religion of hope, restoration, grace, and redemption.

God's grace is known to most of us as unmerited favor, something that we cannot pay for or even earn. Grace is what saves us and what is sufficient for us when we are still wretched within the strongholds of Satan. This action word known as grace is often considered divinely distributed and divinely understood no matter what lifestyle you are a part of; grace is always relevant. Yes, this five-letter word, *grace*, spans throughout time and centuries as a word that has changed lives and situations.

Today, we must be mentally and emotionally prepared to receive and accept the grace that God has given us. The power of God's love and grace shifts the paradigm from no favor to supernatural favor when it rests, rules, and abides with us. As we continue to grow as servants of God and believers in Christ, an invitation and rededication must be made so that God's power can rest, rule, and abide with us. Also, as we develop a prayer life through becoming willing vessels so that He abides within us daily, we must also abide with Him through the Holy Scriptures so that others who do not know how to pray can see the "good" spirit dwelling within each of us. God wants us to know that He still loves us and wants us to love Him in return. All that is required is for us to believe in His love, mercy, and grace.

As we take this journey together, it is my prayer that God will reveal Himself through the pages of this book. And may the Holy Spirit rest in each of your hearts, the sanctified remnants of scriptures that will help you resist the vices of the devil, or the people who are possessed by his demons that try to obstruct and steal your joy and kill your zeal to serve the Most High God. This book intends to outline scripture and extra biblical writings from scholars and teachers who succinctly propose that an individual who desires to know God can know Him without the "pomp and circumstance" of religion.

Additionally, it is my prayer to show that the Bible is written proof to mankind that we were created by intelligent design. It states that God spoke into existence everything by commanding these words

"Let there be ... ," and at the end of the creation, He saw that "*it was very good*," Genesis 1 (NKJV) yet the common question that has remained constant for everyone at some point in their lives is "Why were we created and what is my purpose?"

In the past, we've learned and trusted in whatever academic curriculum that we were taught in school as knowledge that is guaranteed to be true and with merit. We believe in the authors and publishers of our math, science, and history books; we believe in the writings of Aristotle, Plato, and Einstein so greatly that we will pay hundreds of thousands of dollars to become a professional in explaining the ideals or processes that these great people developed.

But the historical relevance and accurate correlations between world, ancient, and natural history in the Bible have always been the leading causes of debate or wars in the world down through the centuries. Consequently, the written passages of the Old Testament and New Testament writings for the Christian faith have been looked upon with deep speculation and disbelief. That's why it is important for each of us to believe that our worship and praise helps us to remain connected to a belief that there is a greater hope and assurance during times of trouble. There is a "celestial being" that desires to grant us immeasurable peace which will surpass all of our understanding, but we must seek that peace with our whole hearts in total commitment. We call this "celestial being" GOD, our Creator—this type of commitment means that we are totally and freely decreasing our natural thoughts and hopes of our personal gains or prestige within our respected communities to become spirit-filled vessels of joy, faith, and love through the power of the Holy Spirit.

This is my prayer that this book will raise fundamental discussions of what is the significance of understanding who is The Christ, The Messiah, The Redeemer, and The Atonement? I decree that this book will open dialogue to these questions and personally correlate them toward eternal life in an individual perspective. I also pray that you allow the Holy Spirit of God to connect to your spirit and reveal who Jesus Christ is and how to understand the true message of His teachings and not the teachings of men. Understanding this, prayerfully, will provide traction so that you can believe that you are loved and were created with a divine purpose preordained by God. However, the only way you can do that is to be connected to the supernatural Grace and Hope that is waiting for you.

HOPE

"My People"

Through the centuries I have loved your forefathers
I have blessed
There are everlasting promises
Search for me with your heart, walk in my precepts, show me
your devotion
I'm still in the midst I created the universe and all mankind
My word was written to instruct
I am God
I speak life and I ordained the laws if you are in doubt about
my existence
Start by reading my word
Reflect back to how you got here, I have never left you
Nor forsaken you
I have chosen you in spite of your wickedness
If you believe, accept the truth
I am God
You are the descendants of my promise
I will pour when you exalt and obey my word

© 2004 *"Naima's Inspirational Melodies"*

CHAPTER ONE

God's Plan for Us

"For whom He foreknew, He also predestined *to be* conformed to the image of His Son, that He might be the firstborn among many brethren. [30] Moreover whom He predestined, these He also called; whom He called, these He also justified; and whom He justified, these He also glorified. [31] What then shall we say to these things? If God *is* for us, who *can be* against us?" Romans 8:29-31 (NKJV)

When (Yahweh) God chose Abraham and blessed his seed to be a great nation, his lineage established the Monotheistic culture that announced the worship of the One True God, Yahweh (God). From this lineage birthed the nation of Israel, who was chosen by Yahweh to be the nation of people that would one day reconcile the other nations who worshiped pagan deities back to Him. Consequently, this meant that the chosen people of Israel had to become a "set apart" nation that lived and existed differently than the nations that worshipped the gods Asherah, Astarte, and Baal.

Over 800 years before the writings of the Old Testament scriptures in Leviticus and Deuteronomy, God first communicated with Abraham in Genesis 12 that Abraham's seed would bless all the families of the earth; all that Abraham had to do was act in obedience to God's calling (Genesis 12:1–3). Consequently, through Abraham's obedience, he would reveal the nature of God to other nations who continued to live a life of evil and wickedness. The Children of Israel are the descendants of Abraham whom God had chosen to be that Holy Nation and Royal priesthood. God required that they adhere to all the laws and commandments that accentuated the spirituality and close connection to a God who is more powerful than all other gods on earth. However, their transition was very difficult and almost impossible to achieve. They endured slavery, wandering in the wilderness, and eventual captivity because of their constant disobedience to the leadership of Yahweh.

Eventually, the children of Israel were delivered from the bondage of Pharaoh by God with the help of Moses as their natural leader, who communed with God to convey the blessings of obedience when they were in complete alignment with God's plan. Also, Moses delivered the curses of disobedience if they disobeyed God's plan to be holy. During this time, there wasn't an established way of accomplishing these moral, civil, and ceremonial characteristics, so Yahweh spoke into existence a sacrificial system and a love and loyalty system that we now have today as seen in the chapters of Leviticus 26 (Sacrificial System) and Deuteronomy 28 (Love and Loyalty). Both chapters outline God's laws and understandings that people who believe in the one true God can read to better understand the true nature and character of God. The true nature of God was revealed in the Old Testament scriptures of Leviticus 26 to prepare the children of Israel for their entry into the promise land and to understand that Yahweh's purpose for them was to reveal His providence on all mankind.

Let us consider God's requirement of mankind's unquestionable obedience and divine plan and purpose for us. Leviticus 26 tells us that Israel's acts of disobedience would lead to the complete loss of their distinct identity and purpose that God had for their lineage. However, it is important that we continue to strive for sanctification and holiness by understanding that our lives are supposed to be beacons of the blessed assurance of God's covenant with Abraham that He would bless Abraham's seed from generation to generation because of their sanctification through obedience. That's why it was so important for God to reiterate to the Israelites that they were to walk in holiness and keep His statues, and in return, He would be their God. But they had to be sanctified by obedience.

The entire book of Leviticus has very necessary significance because it helps the readers of the Old Testament refrain from being confused about the different sacrificial rituals that the Old Testament covers by other biblical, historical, and prophetic chapters in the Bible. Additionally, when we look comparatively at Leviticus 26—just like Deuteronomy 28—it strongly emphasizes that there are consequences warranted through disobedience and treachery, as well as blessings in following God's laws and commands. Yahweh chose the descendants of Abraham, whom are the Israelites, to function as His leading example of holiness and obedience to other nations. He essentially wanted them to be considered by other nations as a "holy nation." And He wanted to show others that this can only come through willing obedience and submission to God's plan.

Additionally, God chose a Hebrew named Moses to lead them into their divine destiny. Moses was instrumental in proposing a system of regulations that would sustain a life of blessings, but it would only be a blessing if the Israelites would accept God as the true living God. God revealed Himself through signs and wonders while they were in bondage in Egypt by showing His power over the Egyptian gods with the ten plagues as He controlled the water, insects, air, sky, and life. Yahweh wanted the world to know that He is "I AM," meaning He is the Creator of all things, and He wanted to assure the Israelites that there is no other God mightier than He is.

However, throughout the journey of the Israelites in the wilderness, they continually doubted and complained whether or not they were in safe hands with Moses and Yahweh and sought ways to worship gods they'd grown accustomed to while in bondage in Egypt. Yet Yahweh continued to speak to them and reveal to them that He loved them and would bless them if they would turn from the idols and sanctify their hearts and minds to Him. Moses illustrated the book of Leviticus to them to teach them about holiness, sanctification, and justification by Yahweh's standards. But it was too difficult for them to turn from their wicked ways and submit themselves to Him. We see that Moses wanted them to know, through the book of Leviticus, that God could not be bribed or manipulated by human actions. God required that they be holy and prepare themselves to be the vessels of salvation and holiness for future nations.

Moses addressed the people of Israel on numerous occasions in what appeared to be sermons of frequent exhortations and overemphasis on living according to God's call for obedience. The significance of Deuteronomy 28 specifically speaks on total acceptance of living a holy life under the guidance of God. Deuteronomy was written to help the Israelites maintain a holy relationship with God after they entered the promise land. It was God's way of ensuring that they would continue to reveal the love and desire for all mankind that He has for them. Deuteronomy also reveals that God is merciful and a God of second chances. But God requires our obedience to His plan and purpose for holiness; holiness is paramount in the life of a person who desires a relationship with God. Although we may want to believe that equal emphasis would be to provide a balanced synopsis of the blessings of obedience and the curses of disobedience, this is not the case.

The curses of disobedience were expressed in more detail because of the constant disobedience of the Israelites and their need to seek other gods for their protection. God wants everyone to know that obedience ensures divine blessings in terms of material prosperity and national security, while disobedience will have opposite consequences that will lead to a disconnection from having a blessed relationship with God. In conclusion, Deuteronomy 28 and Leviticus 26 were significant to the Israelites as they provided a before, during, and after understanding of God's plan for them to become the chosen nation that would ultimately reconcile all peoples back to the divine alignment that we were created in prior to the induction of sin through Adam and Eve.

Leviticus 26 points to a moral code of living that reveals how God cares and wants to dwell with us. Also, the overall book of Leviticus was God's direct conversation to the children of Israel which expressed holiness, love, and obedience. God wanted them to know that they would be victorious over their enemies and not lack for anything, but they had to give their lives and hearts in obedience to Him. God wanted them to remember each of the covenants that He had made with Abraham, Isaac, and Jacob, which encompassed blessing their seeds if they acknowledged Him always as their God (Lev. 26:42–44). Also, the priesthood in Leviticus points ahead to the mediator, Jesus Christ, who would once and for all reconcile sinful man to a holy God.

Leviticus 26 reiterates that God is a jealous God and holiness is necessary in order to come to Him with an offering of sacrifice or praise. God would no longer accept mankind's unacceptance of Him as omnipotent. God stated in Leviticus 26:1 (NKJV) that "I *am* the Lord your God," meaning He still loves them and will forgive them but hates the sin and disobedience that they may do. Deuteronomy 28 expressed to the children of Israel that they would be blessed and experience many blessings of God's promise when they were in obedience to His will. However, it also expressed that they would become a disobedient nation who had to endure judgments and calamities over and over because of their blatant disobedience. But at the end, God would allow them to once again possess the land that was promised to them and ultimately fulfill their destiny as the lineage of the Messiah.

The children of Israel, by now, fully understood who God was and the requirements He desired. It was just a matter of time for them to fully and obediently embrace Him as their God and provider. Even today, God's requirements to be holy comprise of becoming "set apart" and consecrated from the pleasures and thoughts that may prohibit a person from remaining faithful and true to Him. In other words, a person must make a committed effort to live a life that reveals the true nature of God, and the only way that we can achieve this is through a spiritual transformation within our hearts to accept God as Father and Christ as Savior and be filled with the Holy Spirit.

CHAPTER TWO

Now Is the Acceptable Time

"We then, *as* workers together *with Him* also plead with *you* not to receive the grace of God in vain. For He says: 'In an acceptable time I have heard you, and in the day of salvation I have helped you.' Behold, now *is* the accepted time; behold, now *is* the day of salvation. We give no offense in anything, that our ministry may not be blamed. But in all *things* we commend ourselves as ministers of God: in much patience, in tribulations, in needs, in distresses, in stripes, in imprisonments, in tumults, in labors, in sleeplessness, in fasting; by purity, by knowledge, by longsuffering, by kindness, by the Holy Spirit, by sincere love, by the word of truth, by the power of God, by the armor of righteousness on the right hand and on the left, by honor and dishonor, by evil report and good report; as deceivers, and *yet* true; as unknown, and *yet* well known; as dying, and behold we live; as chastened, and *yet* not killed; as sorrowful, yet always rejoicing; as poor, yet making many rich; as having nothing, and *yet* possessing all things." (2 Corinthians 6:1–10; NKJV)

Can you remember the time when you first understood what being a Christian really meant? Can you remember your first spiritual encounter with the Holy Ghost? I can. But first I would like to address my first question: What is Christianity? I used to think that it was my thoughts and actions and how I was identified while growing up. I thought that Christianity was the first and only religion ever created and that no one and nothing else was more relevant than following what I was being taught by my pastor and fellow church members. After realizing that I was very naïve to think that Christianity was the first religion, I started to seek a more detailed and succinct understanding of my faith. I wanted to read or view everything that I could find about Christianity, different faiths, who was Jesus, and the disciples.

I later found out that there are many interpretations of who Jesus is and what His true purpose was on earth. Some historians believe that He was only a carpenter's son. Some say that He was a prophet and a militant who wanted to liberate His Jewish people from the bondage and persecution of the Roman Empire. Then, some truly believe that He is the Son of God and was sent to earth to redeem mankind because of our inability to effectively make a choice to be reconciled back to our Creator. Those who believe that Jesus is the Son of God made a conscious choice to believe and have faith that Jesus is more than just a carpenter's son, a prophet, or a militant who wanted to liberate His Jewish people; we believe that Jesus is the fulfillment of prophecies foretold over four hundred years prior to His birth.

It is believed that He has been given the authority and power by the Creator of all things to heal those that are sick of all diseases and to restore love, peace, and joy in the hearts and lives of anyone who would accept His teachings of love, salvation, and peace into their hearts and, more importantly, be willing to share the good news that we are all loved by God. However, there was a careful stipulation that was required. This stipulation was easy to understand but hard to accept.

Being a Christian means that we have accepted Christ as our personal Savior and that we've agreed deep in our hearts to walk according to His teachings. Paul spoke to the Philippian church and told them to "Let this mind be in you, which was also in Christ Jesus" (Philippians 2:5; NKJV). Christ never boasted that He was equal to God (His Father), nor did He attempt any opportunities to build a reputation of supreme honor and social status to make others worship Him or fear Him. He never attempted to forcibly tell someone to submit to Him; on the contrary, Christ exhibited the complete opposite.

He took the form of a servant-messenger to walk from city to city, talking and greeting those that were considered castaways and people whom society and the government deplored. His exhibition of humility and inclusiveness to all men and women stirred up feelings of rebuke and resentment among those that professed to be men of God, keepers of the law, and doers of good for the people. That's why it's important to understand the significance of the scripture as it says that Christ "was made in the likeness of men" (Philippians 2:7 NKJV). Christ wanted all men to know that He was human and divine at the same time.

This is revealed in scripture as Christ being divine when we read John 1:1–4 (NKJV): "In the beginning was the Word, and the Word was with God, and the Word was God. He was in the beginning with God. All things were made through Him, and without Him nothing was made that was made. In Him was life, and the life was the light of men." Additionally, scripture reveals the natural birth of Christ, as it reads in Isaiah 9:6 (NKJV), "For unto us a Child is born, unto us a Son is given; and the government will be upon His shoulder. And His name will be called Wonderful, Counselor, Mighty God, Everlasting Father, Prince of Peace." Also, in Matthew 1:23 (NKJV), it reads, "Behold, the virgin shall be with child, and bear a Son, and they shall call His name Immanuel,' which is translated, "God with us."

Many anti-Christians believe that Jesus was only a man and, at best, just a prophet, but throughout the Old Testament biblical text, it concisely outlines the birth, death, burial, and resurrection of the Savior many years before Jesus's birth. Also, in the Old Testament writings, there are three hundred fifty prophecies that were fulfilled when Christ died; there were forty-four Messianic prophecies fulfilled as well.

It is important to remember that Jesus had to be made perfect flesh and of human origin in order for the atonement of sin to be perfected and accepted by God. Consequently, the begotten Son of God, the Christ, had to become the Redeemer of the world who was approachable and reachable to everyone, so that the ultimate plan and desire of our Creator can be made known to all mankind. God's ultimate plan for mankind is to worship Him and to live a life eternally that chooses to glorify and magnify Him as Creator.

Additionally, God gave us dominion over everything on this earth; He allowed Adam to name and identify all of the creations that were made by Him. It was, and still is, God's plan to establish us as rightful leaders on earth. However, we cannot take our right place of dominion when we are spiritually disconnected from God. That's why Jesus Christ came to this world. He was born in the likeness of men with human feelings, emotions, and compassion; however, what separated Christ was His compassion and mission to love and save everyone by telling them that their Father in heaven loves them and wants them to build a personal relationship with Him by accepting Him as their Redeemer and Savior. Some individuals are considered to be castaways from society who have made decisions in their lives that reveal, quite frankly, they are messed up. Unfortunately, they are branded with a scarlet letter *S* for "shameful" that they were no longer worthy or accepted among "regular" people. Today, we find ourselves at a pivotal moment in our lives where we have to make a choice to present ourselves in the likeness of Christ so that our lives can draw those that feel hopeless and lost closer to divine reconciliation.

Jesus teaches us in Matthew 7:1 to "Judge no one" and that we are to refrain from looking at others with a judgmental temperament and a self-righteous attitude. There is a story in the Bible found in John 8:1–11 that tells about a woman who was caught in the act of adultery; the community and a religious leader of that time grabbed her, took her to Jesus, and proclaimed to Jesus, "Teacher, this woman was caught in the act of adultery." The ruler wanted Jesus to know that according to the established laws and traditions, the woman should immediately be stoned to death for breaking a moral law. Jesus, during this time, began to inscribe words in the dirt. The accusers of the woman were standing there demanding an answer from Jesus to affirm and sentence her to death, but instead, Christ simply asked a question: "Let the one who has never sinned, throw the first stone!" When the accusers heard this, they began to walk away one by one. Jesus looked at the woman that was brought to Him and asked her, "Where are your accusers? Are there anyone around to condemn you? She answered, "No Lord." And He told her, "Neither do I, go, sin no more."

This is a powerful example of the grace and mercy that God through His Son has for each of us who have fallen short of God's glory. Each of us has sinned and fallen short of the plan and purpose God has for our lives; we are sinners by nature who need redemption and restoration from the inheritably sinful characteristics that we are born with. Jesus showed us in His actions just how compassionate His love and grace are toward each of us when He said, "Neither do I." He looks beyond our faults and our despair to build a bridge of compassion and love that gives us total peace and blessed assurance that He is with us when everything has gone haywire in our lives. He spoke with authority and encompassing grace to let everyone know that "I am the way, the truth, and the life" (John 14:6; NKJV). This is why Jesus dwelled and walked among those that were sick, hungry, and ostracized by society: to bring them hope, help, and, most of all, healing.

Some people may doubt the divineness of Jesus and believe that He was only a man or carpenter, but how can they dispute any of the writings that existed prior to His birth? Jesus fulfilled the prophecy written in the book of Isaiah 61:1–2 (NKJV) when He proclaimed and affirmed to a Jewish crowd that "The Spirit of the Lord God is upon me; because the Lord hath anointed me to preach good tidings unto the meek; he hath sent me to bind up the brokenhearted, to proclaim liberty to the captives, and the opening of the prison to them that are bound; to proclaim the acceptable year of the Lord, and the day of vengeance of our God; to comfort all that mourn."

You see, Jesus wasn't afraid to stand in the authority and purpose that He was created in. He wanted the Jewish people to know that He was the long-awaited Messiah that they had been praying

for ever since the Intertestamental Period. The nature of Christ wanted to reveal that our time is now to help those that are lost and hurting. One of Jesus's sermons outlined His heavenly truths called "The Beatitudes." Jesus spoke nothing but blessings, hope, and peace into the lives of the people who heard Him affirm:

> Blessed *are* the poor in spirit, for theirs is the kingdom of heaven. Blessed *are* those who mourn, for they shall be comforted. Blessed *are* the meek, for they shall inherit the earth. Blessed *are* those who hunger and thirst for righteousness, for they shall be filled. Blessed *are* the merciful, for they shall obtain mercy. Blessed *are* the pure in heart, for they shall see God. Blessed *are* the peacemakers, for they shall be called sons of God. Blessed *are* those who are persecuted for righteousness' sake, for theirs is the kingdom of heaven. Blessed are you when they revile and persecute you, and say all kinds of evil against you falsely for My sake. Rejoice and be exceedingly glad, for great *is* your reward in heaven, for so they persecuted the prophets who were before you. (Matthew 5:3–12; NKJV)

There is no time to judge or ostracize those who have sinned. Romans 3:23 tells us that "all have sinned and fallen short of God's glory." Therefore, we must seek to be a representative of the Spirit of the Lord in order to be lights that lead the way to repentance and salvation so that, prayerfully, we are planting or watering a seed unto salvation in those that are seeking deliverance. Now is the acceptable time to allow others to see the Christ that dwells within us and not the spirit of the one that is the "accuser of the brethren."

The glory and beauty in understanding this revelation is that we are delivered and set free from the supernatural bondages of our sinful nature when we become living testimonies of hope, deliverance, and salvation through our personal walk with Christ. We are living examples that miracles and exorcisms are still functioning universally in the Christian faith. That's why it is important to never be ashamed of the Gospel of Jesus Christ after accepting Him into your life. Your personal testimony is the living power unto salvation because you are the true revelation of God's power that rests, rules, and abides within your heart. You have been drafted into the service unto the Lord to be the salt and light of the world. God desires that you come to Him as a babe with obedience, faith, and trust for all things. Additionally, as I started to grow in my faith, it allowed me to experience the different doctrines and dogmas of Christianity. I began to see that Christianity is far more than what I first understood as my faith; now I understand that Christianity is a lifestyle that has been changed to reflect a life that reveals kindness, mercy, and forgiveness to those that may or may not deserve it. Another word for these actions is called *Grace*.

In the Bible, there's a passage of scripture that tells us the story of a man who sat at a pool called Bethesda; he was physically unable to move on his own. There were others at this particular pool waiting for a celestial event to happen. At a certain time, an angel would appear and trouble this pool. (The time isn't so much important as the actual event that was happening.) At the acceptable time, the angel came to that location to "trouble the water" (John 5:4; NKJV). When we describe the pool as being "troubled," this is referencing something moving or about to happen in the pool that was being caused by the angel on purpose. Now this pool wasn't very pretty, nor did it have five star amenities; many of the people who gathered there were castaways, hurting, disabled, and in need of natural and supernatural healing or deliverance. How many people do you know who are still waiting for something to move in their lives? They sit in their lives of spiritual poverty and supernatural depravity until they become crippled in their minds, believing that there's no hope and all is lost. They are looking for any sign of a Savior or Anointed One to save them. We must be ready to help those that are seeking change, removing the mask, and looking to God for strength because they have realized that no one can take that leap of faith without help. Oftentimes, the outward appearance or the circumstance that a person is held captive in is not their fault and they really want to escape and be free. We can help because we have the good news! Share it with them and wait to see the goodness of God in the land of the living.

Paul often encouraged and uplifted the early Christians to free their hearts and minds from the bondage of 613 Mosaic Laws and trying to incorporate the customs and characteristics into their worship. He had to remind them that they were saved and reconciled by Christ's death, burial, and resurrection. They were saved from sin by grace through faith and not by the works of good deeds or keeping statues that reveal an outward commitment. Christ came so that we may have life and joy in knowing that our works or positions cannot ensure our salvation. Jesus was very succinct about this when He addressed the scribes and Pharisees on many occasions to let them know that although they were leaders with a title and position in Jerusalem, they were still, in the eyes of God, men that constantly took advantage of their position to enforce their way of life on the Jewish people. In Matthew 23 (NKJV), Jesus speaks to the multitudes about how the scribes and Pharisees "sit in Moses' seat" to tell the people what to observe and do, yet they do not do it themselves. This is a very strong point Christ wanted to make: the scribes and Pharisees wore clean and fine garments on the outside, but their hearts and spirits were dirty.

He wanted us to know that now is the acceptable time to stretch out our hearts, believe, and be baptized with the infilling of the Holy Spirit so that our minds would be transformed and renewed into the divine understanding that we are more than conquerors from our past sins and that we must "press toward the goal for the prize of the upward call of God in Christ Jesus." (Philippians 3:14; NKJV).

Time is running out for those who still believe that there is a specific pattern and program that allows believers in Christ to walk in order to receive eternal life. All the doctrinal discords and denominational strongholds must be broken in order for us to reveal Jesus again to those that are lost. He is the way, not man's laws or man's dogmas. Christianity has been divided so many times due to doctrinal discords or man-made interpretations of the Bible. All the sacrifices and offerings were given and accepted by God through His Son, Christ Jesus, as He willingly became the ultimate sacrifice. He is the "last sacrifice," so let's affirm that salvation for us is free. All we have to do is accept the gift that He has already paid for and freely given to each person that lives, moves, and has their being.

Regardless of your past or lifestyle, God has provided us with an intercessor and advocate to present our spiritual cases for salvation. Jesus told us that we can give Him our sins and guilt and cast all our anxiety and pain on Him because He cares for us. He was wounded for our transgressions and bruised for the sinful acts that we've committed. By the blood that He shed on Calvary's cross from the beatings by the Romans with a whip made of small, sharp daggers, by which every stripe that was beaten on Him, we are healed (Isaiah 53:5). Now is the time to allow our hearts to be emptied and broken from sin and to be renewed, as well as filled with the Holy Spirit. It is God's desire that no one should be lost or die in their sins but accept Christ as Savior and renew their hearts and minds with the Holy Spirit to be governed and sanctioned by grace through faith.

When we accept Christ as our Savior, we begin to walk by faith and commitment that we will start to live a righteous and holy life that embraces the infilling of the Holy Spirit, who abides in our minds and hearts. Many doctrinal believers question whether signs and wonders are still relevant and if there has been a cessation of the Holy Spirit; I used the word *cessation* because this word has been used by many of them to tell believers in Christ that the Holy Spirit and the gifts of the Spirit are no longer active in the Christian church. However, if you research the synonyms of this word, you will find that an alternative word means "pause." So, He is waiting for you to take your hearts and minds off "pause" and seek Him. Invite Him into your heart and life today so you can start to feel the peace and joy that has substantial healing power.

During the Apostolic age of the church and during the Empirical age of the church, the Holy Spirit was still very active in each believer. Since the Day of Pentecost, the Holy Spirit has been poured out on all men who believe; additionally, it is important to acknowledge that the promise of Christ told everyone not to worry or be alarmed because He was ascending to prepare for the homecoming of those that believed and accepted Him. He stated with authoritative affirmation, "But you shall receive power when the Holy Spirit has come upon you; and you shall be witnesses to Me in Jerusalem, and in all Judea and Samaria, and to the end of the earth" (Acts 1:8; NKJV). The importance of this affirmation from the Savior is that miracles, signs, and wonders were still being performed and deliverance was still happening well after Christ's ascension.

The church began to grow and tell everyone about the risen Savior and His promise to return. This was also during the times of the greatest opposition and persecution of the Christian believers as well. There were believers that were killed for their faith and given the

Christian name as martyrs; many were used as gladiators or coliseum spectacles for the enjoyment of the emperors of that time. Yet it was through their faith and belief in Jesus that they were able to endure all persecution to continue to spread the good news of salvation. As a result, it was the Holy Spirit that rested and ruled within each of them that gave them hope and peace to withstand persecution and eventual death for their faith. It wasn't until the fourth century that Christianity became accepted by the Roman leadership of Emperor Constantine, which ultimately led to Christianity being the official religion of the Roman Empire. However, it was after the official acknowledgement of Christianity and eventual institutionalization that the Holy Spirit slowly paused from the Christian faith.

Consequently, small groups and functions of believers and hearers of the teachings were still exhibiting the power of the Holy Spirit and the gifts of the Spirit in a more pure and primitive form outside the institution of the Christian church. This was the acceptable way and time that the Holy Spirit continued to flow and manifest His authority in all those that truly believed without prejudice. This is still true today; we must remember that when man's position and authority gets in the way, the Spirit of God option's not to flow until the hearts and minds are turned completely to Christ. The Lord wants us to continue to believe and receive the gift of the Holy Spirit, but we have to allow ourselves to be living sacrifices, holy and acceptable to God, we cannot be effective without the infilling and anointing of the Holy Spirit to abide in our lives.

Everyone has a specific mandate to walk and grow as an ambassador for our faith; now is the acceptable time to expand our faith and calling to be "beacons of life" and prosperity that gives all the glory to God for the blessings and provisions that we have today. The tender mercies of unmerited favor that we have been given should bring us closer to accepting the fact that we are nothing without Christ, but with Christ, we are more than conquerors.

CHAPTER THREE

I Lift My Hands

"What shall I render to the Lord *For* all His benefits toward me? I will take up the cup of salvation, and call upon the name of the Lord. I will pay my vows to the Lord Now in the presence of all His people. Precious in the sight of the Lord *Is* the death of His saints. O Lord, truly I *am* Your servant; I *am* Your servant, the son of Your maidservant; You have loosed my bonds. I will offer to You the sacrifice of thanksgiving, And will call upon the name of the Lord." Psalm 116:12-17 (NKJV)

I remember as a teenager growing up in church being called to the altar by the pastor for prayer. The musician was playing a melodic tune on the B3 Hammond organ, and the drummer was keeping the rhythmic beat in a two-step vibe. There were about four of us that walked up to the altar to stand in front of the pastor as he asked us, "Do you believe that God sent His Son and that Jesus is the Son of God?" "Yes," I decreed. Then, the pastor, along with the missionaries and deacons, told me these four words: "Lift up your hands." I slowly lifted my hands, and as my arms started to raise, I felt a sense of vulnerability and exposure to my entire body. I didn't like the feeling at all; it seemed as if all eyes were watching me and I was the center of attention at that moment while my hands were raised and while I was facing the altar. This revealed to everyone there that I was willingly surrendering my will to God. As the pastor began to pour and rub the olive oil into his hands, he rubbed his hands together so that he could evenly smear the oil. Then all of a sudden, he pressed his oil-drenched hands around my head and began to pray. I could feel the words that the pastor started to say: "In the name of Jesus, heal and remove the pain and anger." These powerful words started to attach themselves to my soul slowly and completely.

This type of prayer, called a "Prayer of Submission" to Christ, is a very powerful prayer that reveals to the supernatural world that you are seeking Christ and have surrendered your heart and will to God's love. However, this automatic supernatural submission was disconnected when Adam and Eve fell from God's love, protection, and grace in the Garden of Eden. It was through the first man, Adam, that man was lost and catapulted into sin. Since that time, man has consistently turned his heart away from God's love.

The depravity of sin seems to have become common place in our culture, and with every generation, reprobation and contempt for God's will have grown even more prevalent. That is why a paradigm shift must begin in the hearts and minds of mankind to hear the words of the Lord. It is God's will that none of mankind should perish or be lost but be reconciled back to him. As Christians, we were given a specific command from the Lord during His ascension into heaven to "Go" preach and reconcile the lost back to the Father by teaching them how to accept the good news of salvation, the continued promise of God that we are loved with an everlasting love, and that our reconciliation back to Him is near and attainable. All we have to do is accept Jesus Christ as Savior. Jesus's ministry was divinely ordained to reestablish the will of God to mankind and not the laws of man.

Jesus stated that He did not come to destroy the law (Messianic law) but to fulfill it, and it was with this announcement that He also became the Messiah and the Redeemer to all who will accept Him as Savior and His teachings as a way of life. Jesus was not against any of the laws, nor did He feel that the laws were detrimental to understanding the acceptance of God's will and desire for all mankind. Jesus even correlated the laws when He gave His Sermon on the Mount, which is also called "the Beatitudes," where He began to impart blessings and affirmations into the life of every person under the sound of His voice. These Beatitudes were promises of salvation and grace. The uniqueness of the Beatitudes is that each one of them provided a life application reference to the 613 Mosaic Laws already in place by the Jewish people.

During the time of Christ and early Christianity, there were four different variations of Jewish religious beliefs—the Sadducees, Pharisees, Zealots, and the Essenes—all of which had different views of living acceptably for God. The Pharisees were very strict and required high observance to the Mosaic Laws of the Torah and accepted oral traditions passed down of Jewish customs and rituals; they also believed in the resurrection of the dead. The Sadducees emanated from priestly heritage and kept the Mosaic Law; however, they did not accept oral traditions. The Zealots were the most militant of all the Jewish groups and wanted freedom from all non-Jewish rule. The Essenes were anticipators of the Messiah and believed that the Messiah would return and establish a kingdom back on earth and free the Israelites from bondage.

The Mosaic law did not sustain supernatural peace because it created an atmosphere of fear and insecurity among those that tried so hard to abide by it. The Old Testament scriptures reveal so often how difficult it was for mankind to obey the first two commandments of the Mosaic law as it commands,

> I *am* the LORD your God, who brought you out of the land of Egypt, out of the house of bondage. You shall have no other gods before Me. You shall not make for yourself a carved image—any likeness of *anything* that is in heaven

above, or that *is* in the earth beneath, or that *is* in the water under the earth; you shall not bow down to them nor serve them. For I, the LORD your God, *am* a jealous God, visiting the iniquity of the fathers upon the children to the third and fourth generations of those who hate Me, but showing mercy to thousands, to those who love Me and keep My commandments. (Exodus 20:2–6; NKJV)

Also, our relationship with God requires that we present ourselves in the image and likeness of Him. God is holy and free of sin. So, in order for us to have access to God, we must be without sin and fully following the commandments. But, because we were born as sinners, we will not be able to embrace most of the 600-plus laws and commandments. The Bible tells us that if we break even the least of the commandments of the Mosaic Law, then we have broken all of them and that "all have sinned and fall short of the glory of God" (Romans 3:23; NKJV). Now you see why it was so important that God sent His son, the Redeemer, to intercede for our lives because there was no way that we would ever be good enough to reconcile ourselves back to God because of the sin and broken laws that we inherited.

Centuries later, Christ took man's sin upon Himself to become the intercessor and the way of salvation by willingly sacrificing His life for all mankind who would have faith and believe. Only Jesus gave great blessings and affirmations during the Sermon on the Mount to give hope to an oppressed people. Our praise and worship should continually be in our hearts when we think about the grace and mercy that have been restored to us; we should be ready to give a testimony of praise and honor to the most high God—the God of Abraham, Isaac, and Jacob—because our ancestors were spared from destruction due to their paganistic worship and were given an opportunity to repent.

That's why there has to be a bridge that leads everyone to repentance. Even now, we have to embrace the fact that we are sinners and that we need to have a way that redeems us when we fail to live by the laws of God. During Jesus's ministry, He taught about something that summarized everything we know and understand about our Christian belief: faith. By faith, we can stretch our intellect further outside the natural box to show that our Father, who is in heaven, can and will always answer us when we are covered by the intercession of Jesus Christ.

Christ loved us so much that He wanted to ease our fears and pain; He spoke the words "your faith has made you well. Go in peace, and be healed of your affliction." (Mark 5:34 NKJV) which is the authentication that Christ is Messiah and Lord of all. If we truly believe that He is the Son of God and by our faith we are made whole and brand new, then we need to have faith and believe that we can be saved from ourselves. Scripture tells us that without faith, it is impossible to please God. Your faith is necessary for spiritually elevating your mind and heart above the depravity of sin and shame.

Jesus Christ wanted to extend salvation to those that were hurting and oppressed, regardless of their background or present situation. Christ stressed in His sermons love, forgiveness, and evangelism without restrictions. "Blessed are those who hunger and thirst for righteousness, for they shall be filled" (Matthew 5:6; NKJV). This infilling requires that each of us individually worship and accept the gift of atonement when we worship. That is why we lift our hands to unveil our love and devotion to Christ. Worship is very personal to every individual who expresses it. Lifting hands, singing, praying, and utilizing their God-given gifts and talents for the Lord is what we are created for.

When we lift up our hands in complete surrender, we fully understand that there is no turning around or looking back to former things or circumstances that held us spiritually captive or in emotional bondage. When we worship, it is the surrendering to emotional openness that spiritually decrees we are seeking to be closer to God by building a strong and lasting personal relationship with Christ.

We have to be willing to release the feelings of guilt and shame in order to cleanse our hearts of the feelings that hold our thoughts to our past mistakes and our present situations and allow them to be renewed; Paul tells us in Romans 12:1–2 that our minds and hearts must be transformed from the sinful thoughts and feelings in order to be reconnected to the powerful and sustained love of God in Christ. It is with this renewal of the heart and mind that we begin to endow our souls to produce loving and caring fruits of the Spirit (Galatians 5:22–23).

Christ is waiting to see our hearts, and He is waiting to respond to the emotional unrest and the spiritual bondage that we are in. He wants to speak to your spirit and tell you that He loves you and He died so that you no longer have to suffer in silence or alone in shame. He wants you to know that He is the way, the truth, and the life (John 14:6). Lift your hands in surrender so that Christ can loosen the shackles that oppress and submerge you in shame and so you can loudly hear the voice of the Lord as He lovingly whispers to your heart, for I am easy to love and I will love you back with an everlasting love. Jeremiah 31:3 NKJV

This is the peace that transcends all understanding. This peace is knowing that Christ has our best interests at heart and He is with us. Now, we can lift our hands knowing that there is a way out of our situation and out of depravity—Christ is that way. However, we cannot expect to come to Christ without increased opposition or problems. Mankind has sustained a life filled with terrible acts against its Creator. We have become numbed and anesthetized to the depravity of sin and disobedience. Just as in the days of the Roman Empire, there's an influx of sexual deviations, false worship, divination, mysticism, and immorality that has allowed men and women to indulge in their ultimate fantasies without feelings of guilt, shame, or remorse.

We have grown into a politically correct nation that once tried desperately to live by Christian principles. We believed that marriage should consist of one man and one woman in order to procreate and multiply upon the earth. We cannot become complacent to alternative living that eliminates the social aspect of procreation. We cannot condone the approval of inappropriate and consensual killing. Just think, if it were not for procreation, many of us would not be here to later fight to maintain this precious gift from God.

Ancient civilizations worshipped idols without feeling that they were angering God by having other gods before Him. Mankind has stamped a blanket approval on immoral acts of violence and terrorism against communities with guns. Cities in the United States have fallen short of God's glory by allowing in sinful people whose only understanding of life is to destroy life. Some cities have become numb to the violence that enslaves it. The children have been forced to live with gun violence in the schools, playgrounds, and even the neighborhood streets; this is slowly becoming an epidemic of pandemic proportions. One could argue that if guns and weapons were not so easily to obtain, then there would not be massive killings and mayhem on the streets and in public places. However, what about the moral and spiritual statues? Can it be that we stopped worshiping God in spirit and truth? The biblical teachings clearly tells us that the very fabric of our existence has been built on our desire to be "like God" or "godlike," and this has separated us from God's love.

The fabric of our Christian values has unseemly diminished among our "peacemakers" as well. There has been an influx of shootings and corruption within the ranks of our people in uniform. These are people whom society has entrusted with the authority to serve, protect, heal, and inform the American people, yet there are small entities that have abused their position and disobeyed God's holy ordinance written in Exodus 20:13–16 (NKJV): "You shall not murder. You shall not commit adultery. You shall not steal. You shall not bear false witness against your neighbor."

The Founding Fathers of this country were Christian believers who established this country based upon the principles of the Moral Laws of the Ten Commandments; although they weren't perfect people, their intention for this nation was. We must find a way to reinstitute the moral laws back into our personal and societal structure. Also, Jesus spoke concise and revolutionary proclamations when He boldly proclaimed, "Blessed *are* those who hunger and thirst for righteousness, for they shall be filled. Blessed *are* the merciful, for they shall obtain mercy. Blessed *are* the pure in heart, for they shall see God. Blessed *are* the peacemakers, for they shall be called sons of God. Blessed *are* those who are persecuted for righteousness' sake, for theirs is the kingdom of heaven" (Matthew 5:6–10; NKJV). I love the perspective of Christ as He was trying to comfort the people in knowing that they were not alone and that the Father was again with them. God has a plan for everyone. His plan may not be as clear for some, but His desire to love us has been proven from generation to generation regardless of our mistakes or inability to fully give ourselves to Him.

In the twenty-first century, we have what's called "social media," which has become one of the many tools of depravity. I say this because through social media such as Facebook, YouTube, and Instagram, people are sharing violence and sin easily and with thousands. I can recall growing up in the eighties and nineties reading and watching the nightly news that often depicted violence and sin as "breaking news" or "important news" of that evening. Many of us would listen and watch with horror and fear when we learned that someone was killed, raped, beaten, or killed by gunshot. We would often believe that the person had to have been temporarily insane or completely insane to act out in such a reckless way toward another human.

It was hard to hear of someone being shot or found murdered on the streets of our community because we were supposed to be a community of believers, a nation founded on the biblically Christian moral laws of the Ten Commandments, one of which specifically states, "You shall not murder" (Exodus 20:13; NKJV). It was God's intention for mankind to live in peaceful harmony and love, but through the centuries, we have developed ways of living with anger and hatred for reasons that include race, ethnicity, and gender. But the greatest reasons many steal, kill, and destroy is because of the evil sin-nature that we were born with. We have not fully understood that each of us have shortcomings; all of us are different and have been uniquely made for the purpose and perfect will of God.

Once we become motivated with this truth in Christ, we can start the process of lifting our hands in total surrender to God's will and plan for our lives. God wants all mankind to believe and love Him just as much as He loves us. He also told us that He loves us so much that He wanted to give us another opportunity to get to know who He is through the resurrection of His Son, Jesus Christ. 2 Chronicles 7:14 (NKJV) tells us, " if My people who are called by My name will humble themselves, and pray and seek My face, and turn from their wicked ways, then I will hear from heaven, and will forgive their sin and heal their land."

God loves mankind so much that He gave His only Son, Jesus, who willingly became the holy atonement for the sins that separated mankind from Him in order to reconcile all mankind back to the Creator (God). So you see, God is allowing mankind time to freely return to its first love. He wants all of us to have an opportunity to be free from sin and evil so that we can whole heartily say, "Our Father, who is in heaven." Yes, I accept Jesus as the willing atonement and sacrifice for my sinful ways so that I may humbly come to repentance for my evil ways, my bad habits, and my personal rejection of Him.

I lift my hands in total surrender to You, Jesus, to ask You to forgive me and come into my heart. I accept You as my Lord and Savior. I believe that You died for my sins and through Your death, burial, and resurrection, You "loved" my sins away. And it is by faith I believe that You are the Son of God and that You love me. In Jesus name, amen.

CHAPTER FOUR

I Surrender All

"Have mercy on me, O God, according to your unfailing love; according to your great compassion blot out my transgressions. Wash away all my iniquity and cleanse me from my sin. For I know my transgressions, and my sin is always before me. Against you, you only, have I sinned and done what is evil in your sight; so you are right in your verdict and justified when you judge. Surely I was sinful at birth, sinful from the time my mother conceived me. Yet you desired faithfulness even in the womb; you taught me wisdom in that secret place. Cleanse me with hyssop, and I will be clean; wash me, and I will be whiter than snow. Let me hear joy and gladness; let the bones you have crushed rejoice. Hide your face from my sins and blot out all my iniquity. Create in me a pure heart, O God, and renew a steadfast spirit within me." (Psalm 51:1–10; NIV)

S urrendering in any situation is a process for anyone to contemplate. Regardless of a person's background, lifestyle, race, or belief, it is very difficult for a person who has freewill to adjust their way of thinking to allow something or someone else to shape and redirect their lives. Also, so much emphasis has been placed on "praying the sinner's prayer" and being baptized in the fire of the Holy Ghost that these manifestations are assurances that a person has surrendered their lives to Christ, but what about the surrendering of their personal will and emotional will to be renewed through the

Spirit and will of Christ? Many new Christians don't know the first thing about the intricacies of salvation and living for Jesus.

It is the job of the true believer to instruct and teach new babes in Christ what it means to live a life that pleases God and mirrors Christ. Paul says it best in scripture that we must study to show ourselves worthy and knowledgeable in our faith as stated in 2 Timothy 2:15. We must also be willing to speak and give a reasonable answer as to why we believe so that others may understand who Christ is. When we say *reasonable*, this means that we should be able to discuss and expound on the three *W*'s of our beliefs. The first *W* is "WHAT is Christianity?" The second *W* is "WHY do you believe that this is the only way to heaven?" And the third *W* of your belief is "WHO is Jesus?" This takes a personal commitment to studying the Bible, praying, and seeking the Holy Spirit's guidance in our daily lives. This takes surrendering all to be transformed and renewed in our hearts and minds to the teachings and governance of the Holy Spirit to rest, rule, and abide in our hearts.

The early church was comprised of people who didn't mind surrendering all to the belief that Jesus Christ is the Savior of the world and the Messiah of the Jewish nation. This also means that we are willing to stand on the teaching that we are no longer bound by the supernatural laws of sin but the sustainment of obedience and contrition. The apostle Paul talks about the supernatural laws of sin in Galatians 5:16–21 (NKJV) when he states to the Christians of Galatia,

> I say then: Walk in the Spirit, and you shall not fulfill the lust of the flesh. For the flesh lusts against the Spirit, and the Spirit against the flesh; and these are contrary to one another, so that you do not do the things that you wish. But if you are led by the Spirit, you are not under the law. Now the works of the flesh are evident, which are: adultery, fornication, uncleanness, lewdness, idolatry, sorcery,

hatred, contentions, jealousies, outbursts of wrath, selfish ambitions, dissensions, heresies, envy, murders, drunkenness, revelries, and the like; of which I tell you beforehand, just as I also told *you* in time past, that those who practice such things will not inherit the kingdom of God.

Unquestionably, when we are free in Christ, we can live in peace and follow Him knowing that we are delivered and set free from them all. We become blessed and supernaturally favored in the Lord. Again, this is one of the teachings of Christ through the Beatitudes, as recorded in the Gospels of Matthew and Luke, when He affirms, through blessing us to be encouraged and surrender the hurt and pain to Him and allow ourselves to live as examples of light and joy to all that are naturally and spiritually oppressed.

It is important to understand that in order for this joyous freedom to happen, each person must individually surrender their hearts to the overall character of Christ. We must also be willing to reveal the teachings of love and service by the way that we live. This is the perfect evangelical understanding of the miracles of God's love and Christ's advocacy for every person that believes. However, we know that false teachings and unholy submissions can destroy a person and leave them in spiritual bondage that will keep them enslaved in emotional and physical service to man, man's laws, and man's principles. Jesus told us that He came into this world so that we can have life, joy, blessings, and peace if only we surrender our hearts and follow His spiritual plan for each of us.

Personally, surrendering all means that I allowed the Spirit of God to fix my heart so that the pain and suffering that once divided and shattered my heart; can be repaired. The shortcomings of our past sometimes hold us back from fully trusting in our spiritual relationship with Christ. Our shortcomings may be revealed at times when we trust the wrong people or when we become entangled in situations that leave us deeply wounded and emotionally scarred. In this present emotional state, we find it especially hard to trust and believe that it is safe to open our hearts to the Lord; therefore, we digress our hearts and emotions to react as people who are hurting and, in return, start to hurt others.

As a young boy growing up on the West Side of Chicago, I remember going to church every Sunday with my mother; we would wake up early in the morning and prepare ourselves to go to church. For me, going to church started out as an exciting activity because it was new, the people there were new, there was music, and everyone appeared to be happy and overjoyed. Although I carried so much anger inside of me as a young boy, I felt something drawing me to want to know God and who this Jesus person was. When I started to attend church regularly, it almost became a ritual and repetitive to me because I understood as a child that this was what we do on Sundays: we go to church to serve the Lord. But I was still seeking the zeal and excitement of others who came that laughed, smiled, and appeared to really be getting so much joy and fulfillment from the service.

My mother would start cooking breakfast, and I could smell the bacon, eggs, and toast cooking. My mother would have an old religious show blaring on the television called *Jubilee Showcase*, and she would sporadically start to hum or brokenly sing along with the church songs and the television. I can still remember as a child feeling that I wanted so greatly to serve God and please Him. However, I didn't fully know who Jesus was. I knew that He was God's son, had died on Good Friday, and had risen from the grave on Easter morning, but that was the overarching extent of my knowledge of Christ. Today, people who desire to know about Jesus have the ability to search and research through technology and other extra-biblical resources in order to form a more defined understanding whether they want to surrender their lives to a religion, tradition, or to a Redeemer.

This is so germane to understanding why we ask others to surrender to the teachings and love of Christ so that they can soon be reconciled back to God. As believers, we must be willing to utilize the technology and extra-biblical resources that are available to us in order to match and effectively evangelize to the unbelievers with a level of understanding to address "where they are the coming from." Paul says it best in 2 Timothy 2:15 (NKJV) when he writes that we should "Be diligent to present yourself approved to God, a worker who does not need to be ashamed, rightly dividing the word of truth." It is our job as believers to be ready to defend our faith with sound and accurate answers. There are many false teachings and information related to Christianity, and it is equally important for every Christian to understand the difference in scripture and heresy or false teaching.

Many people are still caught up in the experience and not the message of salvation. I say that because the experience of salvation can tell a person that there's no need to worry anymore because they have been redeemed or delivered from their sins, or not evangelize to the people who are struggling to maintain their position in the kingdom. Some believers leave that type of situation to the spiritual leaders of their church instead of reaching out, praying, or mentoring their Christian brothers and sisters at their weakest moments.

I've noticed that some believers are so gripped in the experience of service, whereas they are strong "churchgoers" who sing faithfully, teach Sunday school, and are dutiful within their church auxiliary yet fail to grasp the scripture as it tells us in Romans 15:1–4 (NKJV),

> We then who are strong ought to bear with the scruples
> of the weak, and not to please ourselves. Let each of us
> please *his* neighbor for *his* good, leading to edification. For
> even Christ did not please Himself; but as it is written,
> "The reproaches of those who reproached you fell on me."
> For whatever things were written before were written for

our learning, that we through the patience and comfort of the scriptures might have hope.

Some churches are so focused on providing those that come to service with a great show, hook, gimmick, or nugget that they forget to preach and teach the true purpose of the church and the chief cornerstone that every church should be built upon as outlined in Ephesians 2:19–22 (NKJV):

> Now, therefore, you are no longer strangers and foreigners, but fellow citizens with the saints and members of the household of God, having been built on the foundation of the apostles and prophets, Jesus Christ Himself being the chief cornerstone, in whom the whole building, being fitted together, grows into a holy temple in the Lord, in whom you also are being built together for a dwelling place of God in the Spirit.

Additionally, the church is not just a building or a gathering station that has music, people, activities, or missions. The church is within us; it is our foundational belief and commitment to surrender all that is within us for Christ so that His kingdom will be established on earth as it is in heaven. Ultimately, it should be the desire of every man, woman, and child created by God to surrender their hearts and minds to become spirit-filled disciples of Christ's teachings of love, redemption, peace, blessings, surrender, and repentance. Each of us has a spiritual duty to help those that we know are battling the tricks and bondages of the old sinful nature. We are to reach out to them, pray with them, and help them to learn how to encourage and strengthen themselves when the test and trials of their past or current life is gaining ground on their spiritual commitment to live a life that is pleasing to God.

There is more to being a believer or Christian than going to church to "get the Word for ourselves." We must have the untiring compassion for the lost, sick, wounded, and hurt that Christ had for each of us before we accepted Him as our personal Savior. Everyone deserves to know how you were delivered or changed. Share it with them. You may be surprised at the response you get. Remember, God loved us before we loved ourselves. Maybe that person who is hurting or having a hard time pleasing God needs to know that "The Lord has appeared of old to me, *saying*: 'Yes, I have loved you with an everlasting love; therefore with loving kindness I have drawn you'" (Jeremiah 31:3; NKJV).

Instead, we begin a pattern of hurt toward others that desire to be close to us; we lash out in anger and fear of the potential chaos that "might" happen instead of trusting that God loves us, is in control, and has never left us or forsaken us. Our past have a profound ripple effect on everything that we are going to experience in our present lives, which is why it was important for me to internalize Proverbs 3:5–6 because it was the "trust" and "understanding" that God is able to embrace my heart and restore it back to a joyous and peaceful state. All that I had to do was fully let go of the past hurt and shame and forgive those that had emotionally decimated me. But I wasn't healed until I put my life back into God's hands. This was achieved by fully surrendering all the past and present pains and ills to the Creator. I asked Him to restore my joy, and He heard my plea before it was too late. Today, I am a living witness that He has all power to heal, deliver, and set free. If you are seeking peace in your life right now, all you have to do is surrender it all to Him in faith.

You see, I had to surrender my all to Christ because I was a walking corpse who went about life with no true feelings of peace or grace. My past life of service and commitment to my faith became a blur to me because of the way that so many "Christians" were acting around me. Just like them, I would call myself a "Christian" but was not living by the standards that Christ wanted me to live by. It was easier for me to have a drink, use profanity, or even lie to others rather than for me to say, "Lord, I love You." When I look back at that time in my life, I probably caused a lot of people to lose their hope and faith in Christianity. I wasn't that light or salt that Jesus told us to be as believers.

I remember a time when I attended a wedding ceremony and was sitting at a table where everyone began to talk about their jobs and their likes. I listened to the people who revealed that they were nurses, physician assistants, and other professional titles that showed they had a good life. When it was my time to answer what I did, I had to tell them that I drove a fish truck delivering fish to restaurants in the downtown Chicago area. The people looked at me with such a "curious" look. You see, I was wearing a nice suit with nice shoes and was well groomed for the occasion. But those people were who I aspired to become, and not who I really was.

The people sitting around the table immediately stopped talking to me for the rest of the night. The conversation immediately shifted to them talking about the vacations and purchases that they were able to afford. This conversation was a few zeros over my paycheck, and I truly felt as if I were so far over my head and less than the person I was destined to be. But there is a lesson and purpose by God in everything that we experience. I sat there and emotionally endured the way that I was physically and emotionally ignored because of the lack of wealth and position I had in the world. It was the hardest thing for me to endure, but I sat there, ate my banquet food, and didn't say another word.

When I finally left the banquet, I was driving on my way home and began to think about everything that was said. I started to realize that something was missing in my life and that I was not living up to my natural or spiritual potential, meaning I was just surviving here on earth. I didn't have a good job. I wasn't really contributing to make my life meaningful. At this point, everything that I set out to do greater for myself was failing or coming up short. I began to lose hope and believe that this was my life.

I was living in my mother's attic with no future plans of how to do better. I started to undress and get ready for bed. It was a cold night and the attic wasn't insulated, so I had to get extra blankets to wrap up in as I begin to lie down. My mind still raced back and forth through the conversations and emotional feelings from the banquet long after I turned the lights off. My heart started to ache, and I started to sigh heavily more and more until I could not hold back the tears. The cold darkness hid the hurt and pain on the outside, but the inside of me was broken and defeated.

Sometimes it is man, and not Satan, who stands in our lives as the "accuser of the brethren" to constantly reveal to us that we have fallen and are not worthy of God's grace. Biblical-based teachings tell us that grace will lead us safely through; therefore, stand on God's Word as it tells us that all have sinned and fallen short of God's glory and affirms that "I can do all things through him who gives me strength" (Philippians 4:13; NIV). This verse puts in perspective that regardless of where we are in our walk with Christ, He is our first commitment. Our commitment has to first be to Christ and then to ourselves to have faith and trust in the Holy Spirit to lead us into all truth.

Every believer should seek positive, godly fellowship with like-minded believers of their faith for encouragement and accountability. We must be confident in knowing that we are more than just believers of the one true God; but, we are servants of the divine purpose of reconciliation and repentance. Committing to this just and righteous cause helps us to spread hope and love to those that are looking for salvation. Christ is that answer, and through Him we can be victorious. The enemy sends people into our lives to try to destroy our confidence and to make us question if Jesus is who He stated He is. Jesus told us, "I am the way, the truth, and the life," and when we understand that, we can stand boldly on the fact that there is no other name in heaven, on earth, or below earth where a man can be saved but by the name of Jesus. This is why I have peace: I accepted the opportunity to surrender my life and heart to the will of God. Now there is so much peace and comfort knowing that "Jesus has my back" and that I am blessed and supernaturally favored by the Lord.

I am reminded of a scripture in 1 John 1:6–7 as it addresses the subject of fellowship. The passage in 1 John 1:6–7 (NKJV) tells us, "6 If we say that we have fellowship with Him, and walk in darkness, we lie and do not practice the truth. 7 But if we walk in the light as He is in the light, we have fellowship with one another, and the blood of Jesus Christ His Son cleanses us from all sin." The contextual significance that the word *fellowship* in 1 John denotes is referenced only three times within the entire letter; however, *fellowship* is written in conjunction to the *Social-Scientific Analysis* that it was written by John the son of Zebedee in 90–95 AD to the churches in and around Ephesus during a time right after the departure of false teachers. Some believe that they were secessionists who denied that Jesus is Messiah but only human.

So, if you examine closely, we can see that this word is being utilized in two different contexts relevant to the voice of the message. The first word *fellowship* means "fellow" and to be a "participant." It implies fellowship or sharing with someone or in something. The definition of fellowship and its English and Greek meaning are: The Greek transliteration of the word reads κοινωνός and κοινων- in Secular Greek: 1. In Human Life (Friberg, Friberg, and Miller 2005, 233). Thus, when we look at verse 6, we can see the meaning of *fellowship* in the present sense of a person being acknowledged as a willing participant in a belief or activity, they are considered in fellowship. A scripture that further relates to this meaning is Acts 2:42 as it illustrates that "and they continued steadfastly in the apostles' doctrine and fellowship (κοινωνία), in the breaking of bread, and in prayers."

Acts 2:42-47 (NKJV) Greek spelling and lexicon and breakdown of the Greek spelling; according to the *Strong's* Greek breakdown of the word *fellowship* κοινωνός #2841; Plato, of Athens (428/7–348/7 BC), it also means to share with someone in something which he has or "to take part in something which he/she did not have." Additionally, the English definition and pronunciation of this word is fel·low·ship ['felō,SHip], NOUN; friendly association, especially with people who share one's interests. Synonyms: companionship, companionability, sociability, camaraderie, friendship, mutual support, togetherness. Other Biblical passages associated with fellowship and other lexicon versions of the word *fellowship*.[1]

The writer of the book entitled *Handbook of New Testament Exegesis*, Craig L. Blomberg, discusses the fact that "before every exegete turn to secondary literature, it is important that we first "mine" through the New Testament text for clues of historical context in which the word."[3] The word *fellowship* in 1 John 1:5–10 and the writer, John the Apostle, can be further understood within the New Testament scriptures, that Jesus is the "Only begotten son" as disseminated in scriptures such as 1 John 4:9, John 1:14, 18, and John 3:16, 18; God is light (1 John 1:5 NKJV) by earlier writings that he was writing the relevance of divine fellowship of holiness and sanctification of Jesus with God.

Matthew 18:20 also exhibits the importance of fellowship as Jesus proclaims that "For where two or three are gathered together in my name, there am I in the midst." Additionally, John's letter to the churches around Ephesus was written to encourage that there is strength in numbers during persecution and false teaching. Today, it is important to remember that coming together in worship and praise strengthens our faith and through listening to the testimonies of others and praying for strength and discernment through the Holy Spirit with those that we fellowship with, it increases our relationship as corporate believers in Christ and therefore, our fellowship with one another grows more fulfilling and genuine towards everyone around us. Just like the early churches and leaders, who had to endure false teachers and Judaizers. We can admonish their approach to effectively and corporately pray for those that have been weakened by life's tests and troubles and not allow our fellowship with other believers to become discouraged and filled with doubt in the power of two or three gathering in fellowship.

Lastly, the word *fellowship* within the scriptures is further understood as "mutual support" and "togetherness," which the New Testament and the Epistle writer apostle Paul writes in Philippians 2:2 (NKJV), "fulfill my joy by being like-minded, having the same love, *being* of one accord, of one mind.." Paul's decree of his joy would be increased if the believers reinforced the need and desire to come together in fellowship with a spirit of togetherness and mutual support for each other.

CHAPTER FIVE

Jesus Breaks Every Chain

"Now the Lord is the Spirit, and where the Spirit of the Lord is, there is freedom." (2 Corinthians 3:17; NIV)

"The Spirit of the Lord is on me, because he has anointed me to proclaim good news to the poor. He has sent me to proclaim freedom for the prisoners and recovery of sight for the blind, to set the oppressed free, to proclaim the year of the Lord's favor." (Luke 4:18–19; NIV)

The shackles of falling into snares of political correctness, legalism, and traditionalism can sometimes keep us from shouting out to the world, "There is liberty in Christ!" When we get to the point of believing that God is Christ, we must start the process of prayer and consecration to the Lord so that all the restrictions are broken and the restraining yokes are destroyed. This can only be achieved when we allow Christ to become Lord of our lives. We must believe that Jesus is Savior of us all; we must be willing to stand on the facts that He loves us and the unquestionable grace that He continuously exhibits toward us is always acknowledged and appreciated after the veil of truth has been ripped for everyone to see the workmanship of God in Christ. There are so many people who proclaimed to know the perfect will of God and the true way to walking in the will of God, but can they affirm within their hearts that they are renewed from their old destructive habits or disobedient characteristics? This should be profoundly evident in every person who has been transformed in their hearts and renewed in their minds toward the teachings and examples of Christ and is willingly showing love and compassion to those that have been ostracized and physically broken.

People who are physically broken often exhibit parts or portions of their physical appearance that have been damaged in ways that may restrict them from doing things in life that normally would not require help or assistance to accomplish it. We can read in biblical and extra-biblical text from scholars and historians, such as Josephus ben Mattathias, also known as Flavius Josephus (37–100 AD) and Lucian (circa 120 to after 180), that Jesus lived and performed wonders and miracles of healing and deliverance to many people who came to Him for physical healing. It was His compassion and willingness to heal them that affirmed He was more than "just a man"; He was a man fully and divinely sent by God to reveal the omnipotence of God's power working through Him.

Jesus proclaims this in John 14:5–11(NKJV) when a disciple named Phillip questions the divine connection between God and Christ, asking Him to reveal the Father to them. This discussion was happening after another disciple asked, "Lord, we do not know where you are going, how do we know the way?" Jesus said to them, "I am the way, and the truth and the life, no one comes to the father but through me." He was telling them that He and the Father are of one heart and one spirit dwelling in the same body to naturally reveal the unselfish compassion and grace toward all mankind.

Jesus wanted everyone who believed in Him to know that there is peace and security in Him. He stated, "Let not your heart be troubled" (John 14:1; NKJV). Although, He may not physically be in our presence, He is still here and preparing an atmosphere of peace and love that we can share in the fullness of the Father's presence together. Therefore, whatever our problems or vices are, He is here to bring us to a place of salvation and restoration. All that we have to do is give Him our hearts and believe in His love to set us free from the bondages that restrict our belief in His love for us.

However, we can read throughout history about the countless times people who professed to know the will of God and allowed their perception of God in Christ to keep believers of Christ in bondage and spiritual slavery to their interpretations of spiritual love, grace, and mercy. They misrepresented the true foundational spirit of the love that Christ showed when He told His disciples "that where I am, *there* you may be also" (John 14:3; NKJV). Consequently, the examples of inclusiveness of all men were carnally legalized and made very hard to uphold. So often we hear these phrases in ministry: "Submit to authority." "Know your place in the kingdom." "Who is your covering?" "Who did you sit under?" Additionally, when we incorporate the doctrinal teachings, denomination creeds, and overall submission to man's authority, this taints the true nature and ability to fully surrender to the blessings of Christ.

Jesus wanted each of the true believers to know that they are free from the misrepresentations of salvation, deliverance, and devotion to God. He states in John 15:15 (NASB), "No longer do I call you slaves, for the slave does not know what his master is doing; but I have called you friends, for all things that I have heard from My Father I have made known to you." Christ wanted everyone who believed in Him to rely on the inner anointing and discernment of the Holy Spirit to help with teaching and leading others in our faith. Today, many people of faith believe and have taken on the hierarchical teachings that believers need to be "covered" in order to serve God and minister within Christ's body.

Have you been told that you need to be "covered" by a person or religious network in order for your active service in Christ to be honored? Or have you been told that your Christian life may be in severe condemnation and under spiritual disobedience because you are not accountable to someone other than the Holy Spirit? Has this resulted in the fear that without a "covering," you are afraid to minister, preach, pray, or do a myriad of other things you're called to do by the Spirit of God because you will somehow be ministering without protection? This doctrinal discourse began in 1990s and is known as the "Covering Doctrine," which presents itself as a new fundamental doctrine but holds old lies with distinct similarities to the teachings and laws of the Scribes and Pharisees. It is the maintenance of a false system of hierarchical beliefs very similar to a modern-day "pyramid scheme." The teaching on "covering" means that everyone needs to be accountable to someone who is spiritually his or her superior. This may be a group leader, the head of a church auxiliary, your senior pastor, etc. Additionally, these leaders are covered by someone further up the organizational line as well. For instance, a denominational leader can hold the title or office of an apostle or bishop. It is expressed in this doctrine that this is necessary since believers need to be safeguarded from reverting back to sin or teaching the scriptures in error. So, a covering is provided by those who are "more spiritual" to protect "less spiritual" believers from such error. Oftentimes at the very head of this particular pyramid of covering there is a well-known and recognized "leader" who is rarely accessible to new converts and growing Christians of their faith.

Currently, there are several networks offering this kind of covering to those in some form of church leadership or ministry, more often than not for an annual fee. The annual fee usually provides for the running of the network and conferences where you can fellowship with others under your particular brand of covering. You may also be denied entrance from one of these networks because you don't have the appropriate credentials.

This leaves a babe in Christ and new believer with many questions and misunderstandings of the essence of what it really means to be a Christian. Newly born-again believers are often told to attend Bible study and Sunday service in order to continue to grow; however, the time is now to believe that it truly takes more than setting aside two days a week to cultivate and understand our faith. More importantly, it is an ongoing commitment to learning and trusting in the writings and stories of the Bible to internally understand the meaning of spiritual obedience, sanctification, holiness, faith, trust, and salvation.

This newly established hierarchical teaching has severely diminished the authenticity of the true church's mission, vision, and purpose, and for this I apologize to every new believer who has witnessed or been subjected to spiritual bondage and emotional slavery due to this covering doctrine. The Bible clearly teaches in the letters to the Romans, Galatians, and Corinthians that we are free and justified by faith through grace and that God and the spiritual teachings of Christ with the discernment and infilling of the Holy Spirit covers us all.

In the Bible, Jesus also provided us with scriptures that point us in a different direction with regard to our service and worship. In Matthew 20:25–28 (NASB),[5] we read,

> But Jesus called them to Himself and said, "You know that the rulers of the Gentiles lord it over them, and *their* great men exercise authority over them. It is not this way among you, but whoever wishes to become great among you shall be your servant, and whoever wishes to be first among you shall be your slave; just as the Son of Man did not come to be served, but to serve, and to give His life a ransom for many."

Also, in Mark 10:42 (NASB), Jesus tells the disciples that "You know that those who are recognized as rulers of the Gentiles lord it over them; and their great men exercise authority over them."

And lastly, in Luke 22:25–27 (NASB), we read,

> And He said to them, "The kings of the Gentiles lord it over them; and those who have authority over them are called 'Benefactors.' But *it is* not this way with you, but the one who is the greatest among you must become like the youngest, and the leader like the servant. For who is greater, the one who reclines *at the table* or the one who serves? Is it not the one who reclines *at the table*? But I am among you as the one who serves."

The book of Acts clearly outlines the foundational principles and characteristics of the first church. Acts 2:42–47 (NIV) tells us

> "They devoted themselves to the apostles' teaching and to the fellowship, to the breaking of bread and to prayer. Everyone was filled with awe, and many wonders and miraculous signs were done by the apostles. All the believers were together and had everything in common. Selling their possessions and goods, they gave to anyone as he had need. Every day they continued to meet together in the temple courts. They broke bread in their homes and ate together with glad and sincere hearts, praising God and enjoying the favor of all the people. And the Lord added to their number daily those who were being saved."

The people were filled with love, joy, and warm fellowship as they came together as a body of believers to care about each other's circumstances. They encouraged and helped each other when times were tough. They did not look at them with contempt or pity because they were poor or did not have enough goods and money to bring to the community; they loved them and didn't mind helping them. This is a basic foundation of our faith.

Many years after the day of Pentecost when believers received the Gift of the Holy Spirit, the Holy Spirit is the spirit of joy, peace, acceptance, surrender, obedience, and comfort. He is the extension of love from the Father and the Son into our hearts so that we can extend it to those that are hurting and seeking answers to their personal lives. When Jesus met the Samaritan woman at the well, He began to talk to her and minister to her in love concerning her life and situation. He did not follow the tradition of His people and not "have nothing to do with her" because of her lifestyle. Instead, He was more than ready to show her that He is able to love her unconditionally. Now, Jesus knew her past and her present and still wanted to love her into her future. He continued to minister to her and tell her that regardless of what she'd done in her life, she could still be accepted as a person who the Messiah (Christ) can save and forgive.

This was contradictory to the traditional teachings of the Jewish people, but she knew that Jesus was special. His words touched her so deeply that she excitedly ran to tell others about the "Good News" of Christ. She told the other Samaritans, and as a result of her becoming the messenger of the Good news to her people, many others were saved and received the blessings of Christ. This is why it was necessary for every believer to be filled with the Holy Spirit because so many people were being spiritually renewed in their hearts and minds after hearing the Good News of Christ. This Good News did not judge or place restrictions on anyone who wanted to believe and accept Christ as the risen Savior.

Today, people are leaving the legalism of church to pursue a personal relationship with Christ without the stigmas of tradition and doctrine because the behavior and outward emotional appearances of some church people who follow the tradition and legalistic formats are exhibiting the appearances of the Scribes and Pharisees; the only difference is it's the twenty-first century. Our covering should always rest in Christ because the Bible tells us in Matthew 23:8–12 (NKJV), "But you, do not be called 'Rabbi'; for One is your Teacher, the Christ, and you are all brethren. Do not call anyone on earth your father; for One is your Father, He who is in heaven. And do not be called teachers; for One is your Teacher, the Christ. But he who is greatest among you shall be your servant. And whoever exalts himself will be humbled, and he who humbles himself will be exalted." God needs servants in the kingdom who understand that "love and kindness draws" and love hides a multitude of sins" as well. This doesn't mean that living a sinful way is acceptable; it just means that if we show love and patience to those that come to us, then the love of Christ will tear down the strongholds in the heart of that person. We must not make salvation too hard to attain! The penalty and suffering have already been paid through Jesus's death and resurrection.

This is the disconnection between saints, sinners, and "used-to-be saints"; it has divided the kingdom of Christ because the standard has not been upheld due to man's corrupt ways. How can a divided house stand? In the sixteenth century, Martin Luther fought against some of the same things Paul fought against as he started the early churches. Paul and Martin believed that salvation was freely given by Christ through His death and resurrection on the cross, thereby freeing us from works, criteria, and stipulations for salvation. Martin believed what Paul preached: we are all saved by grace through faith and are then justified by faith. We can find this information if we read the biblical books of Hebrews, Romans, and Galatians. Our faith is what makes us whole; our faith is what keeps us connected to our spiritual completeness. Now is the time to start teaching and proclaiming salvation through faith by grace, not works or accepted stipulations of accountability. Surrender to Christ, accept the gift in your hearts, and feel the salvation of the Lord in your lives. It's as easy as saying, "I *believe* (accept as true); therefore, I *receive* (take delivery of). In Jesus name."

One day, I was sitting on a beach in Clearwater, Florida, looking at the tide and sun dancing among all the "Spring Break people" enjoying the sunshine, blue skies, and warm water. The ages of these people varied from three to eighty years old, and they were from all walks of life and of different nationalities. It was wonderful to behold the beauty to see everyone enjoying one thing at one time. But then the Lord brought back to my attention something that I had learned the past year in seminary, which was the fact that most of America's younger generation (Generation Y, Generation Z, or Millennials) no longer believe in God, Jesus, and the Holy Spirit. Additionally, most of the seventeen- to forty-year-olds believe that God is separate from Jesus and that He was a prophet, a carpenter, or just a man. They believe that the Bible was written by men to use and control a person or force them to submit to their (man's) authority. They believe that church is filled with hypocrites and sinners who live equally unsaved lives but appear to be holy only in name and appearance. That is why they don't go to church or believe in Jesus. They believe that there is a God but not the same God that Christians serve. When my wife and I started our ministry, we would often minister and evangelize to individuals who would relay these same feelings and thoughts about "Christianity." However, what surprised us was that most of the people we talked to were former Christians who had fallen victim to "church hurt" or "spiritual bondage," which resulted in that person abandoning their fellowship with God. But what was equally startling was that those people who were "put out of the church" later raised sons and daughters who resent and hate Christianity as well.

You see, Paul said it best as he began to address the issues of spiritual bondage and the false teaching of additional requirements to maintain a proper fellowship with each other as we follow Christ. Paul stated that although Moses hid the glory of God on his face from the children of Israel with a veil, because of the presence of holiness on his face, no man could stand to look upon it and live. Before Christ died on the cross, He spoke to His mother Mary and said to her, "Woman, behold your son!" (John 19:26; NKJV). When you think about it, Jesus was revealing to the Jewish people the glory and salvation of God at that moment. He wanted her, and the disciples with her, to see the birth of living behind the veil of holiness and understanding that now; salvation is free, grace is available, but, more importantly, God still loves His chosen people. Even now, when the scriptures are being read, there is a veil on the hearts of the Judaizers and nonbelievers toward Christ.

That's why so many people have resorted to forming their own type of worship outside the church because it is safer to read scripture and listen to sermons in their homes so as not to risk becoming a victim of spiritual bondage. My wife and I were victims of church hurt, my sisters were victims of church hurt, and countless friends and relatives were as well. We followed the teachings of a pastor and submitted our lives and hearts to the will of the pastor and the doctrines that governed us only to have the spiritual life strangled out of us.

I found myself trying to serve and please the pastor while losing my focus on Christ and His will and purpose for my life. I didn't know how to evangelize to others because I had to ask the pastor if it was all right to speak to that particular person. I even had to ask the pastor if it would be okay to talk and invite certain people to church. And if he said no, then that person was not invited. It truly hurt me to see some pastors and leaders deliberately turn people away because of their looks or present circumstances. They weren't given a chance to accept Christ or even repent. I would ask myself, "What about the Great Commission and the Great Commandment?"

Ultimately, we found ourselves entrenched in the restrictions that held us in bondage to many laws and traditions that kept us from fully embracing the fact that Christ died and took His rightful place as the author and finisher of our faith. He sacrificed His life for our spiritual liberty. You see, Jesus promised us that He would not leave us without a teacher to instruct us about our spiritual power, destiny, peace, and purpose. Paul continued to exclaim that when we come to understand that Christ is our Savior and that He is welcomed in our hearts as an advocate to the Father, then He is the true giver of life, peace, and grace. Therefore, we are spiritually free.

Free means that we are free to trust that the Holy Spirit will lead us and guide us into all truth. The Holy Spirit will comfort us during tough and trying times, and the peace of God will surpass all our understanding and give us peace through Christ Jesus. We cannot fully embrace everything that God has planned for us until we fully believe that the "Lord is that Spirit" and where the Spirit of the Lord is, there is liberty (2 Cor. 3:15–17 NKJV).

It took time for me to fully understand that I was hurt by my church or my connection with men and women who were natural representatives of Christ on this earth. I could not be free from the heartache until I was willing to surrender it to the Lord so that my "liberty" could begin new. Sometimes we encounter people who say that they are lovers of God and men only to see that they are filled with hidden agendas in the name of the Lord.

The first time in my life when I encountered church hurt, I received confirmation from the Lord in a dream that He was calling me to go forth in ministry. I believe that God often calls people into a position where they can be effective for the purpose that He already planned for them. I never considered myself to be a "preacher" or a "hooper" for the Lord. I knew that my passion and strength was to be a leader and a teacher of God's people. I have always enjoyed the way God's Word outlines truths and stories that a person can always relate to everyday life. This is called "life application."

Well, the hurt for me came after I went forth in ministry and began my journey as a minister. The definition of *minister* is to be a servant and someone who is appointed to perform religious services. I was so excited to accept my calling. I studied and prepared myself through prayer, consecration, and being mentored. I knew very influential leaders and pastors in the kingdom of God. There were male and female pastors, and you could feel the anointing of the Holy Spirit in everything that they did. They showed the gifts of the Spirit and walked with charisma and faith that revealed to everyone who saw them, "that they were authorized by the Spirit of God, to walk in this position."

Also, there were leaders and other ministers who could teach the scriptures without hesitation. I also knew men and women of God who everyone knew by name and would automatically be honored when present. You could feel the power of something surrounding each and every one of them. I believe that they were called and chosen by the Holy Spirit to be vessels of His message.

I remember being under the leadership of a pastor who was very wise and knowledgeable about the Bible. He had a real approachable demeanor, and it was so easy to talk and share things with him on all levels of life. I truly enjoyed listening to him and learning from his examples of service and love for others in the body of Christ. We would often go to breakfast and talk about everything! We discussed life, love, people, situations, and, of course, ministry. I learned a lot from him because he wasn't afraid to see me spiritually grow; he wasn't afraid to impart into me as much as possible so that I would not be afraid to stand and proudly proclaim Christ to the world. He understood that it wasn't a race or a competition on how many people would listen and follow us as ministers—it was all about God.

We mutually understood that we were all the same called by God in the commission of souls and to ultimately show godly love and peace to those that don't know that Jesus is the way to peace and joy. He would always smile and be happy to see me and my wife at service. His sermons were so thought provoking and clearly spoken that we didn't need to decipher what God was saying over the yelling, music, or moaning. We were able to be fed the Word so that we wouldn't miss the message from the "angel of the house." I can say with truthfulness and humility that I now pattern my style of leadership from him because this leader wasn't afraid of the enthusiasm and zeal that I had to learn and know. I was a sponge for the Word of God and not the pomp and circumstance of ministry. Thank you, Pastor D. D. Nabor, William Campbell, Jefferson Campbell, and Reverend Harvey Spivey, for allowing me to learn from you and understand that it's all about God and not the individual; and that, mentoring and leadership are always interconnected.

However, I also served under a "man of God" who required that I serve him first and that my loyalty and devotion be only to him without question. He believed that a minister or servant of the Lord should always be submissive under his authority. And if he did not agree with you, you would be forced to sit down and even step down from your position in the ministry. This person would berate you in the pulpit and always tell you that you were "going to Hell." I didn't learn anything tangible from that leader because the message of the cross was often diluted with the accusations of lust, sin, and depravity. There were others in leadership that plainly and blatantly ignored me because I knew that doctrinal teachings and organizational loyalties would often lead to severe church hurt, so they would not have anything to say to me. This was very hurtful and spiritually damaging to me because I was young to ministry, but I wasn't young to knowing Christ.

I was essentially set aside by some because God didn't want me to be damaged spiritually by following the wrong leader. I mean, I was blessed to be under great leadership in my lifetime as a Christian; I've been blessed to sit under the leadership of some leaders who were strong leaders of Church of God in Christ, Pentecostal, Missionary Baptist, and nondenominational. And the correlating truth that I learned after all the surface beliefs was that Christ must be my final submission and final acceptance for true leadership. Now, I understand that everyone has to be willing to be accountable to someone in our faith. I understand that we have to obey those that have rule over us because the Bible tells us that in Hebrews 13:17; but, when does obedience lead to spiritual bondage and eventual spiritual death? It should never happen because the leadership of the body of Christ should always reveal the love of Christ, spiritual humility, and grace that restores, corrects, and encourages those that lend their leadership to them, as service, so that they can be taught how to be effective and spirit-filled disciples who are not ashamed of the Gospel of Christ.

We must understand that everyone is born with leadership qualities and traits, and when we join someone else's mission or vision, we become willing followers of that person's vision and plan. It's not an entitlement because you are in a position. Jesus confronted the leadership of His day when He would often rebuke and correct the Scribes and Pharisees regarding their earthly adornment and prestige, yet Jesus continually used common men and women to spread and share His message. This is the value of a true leader. A leader can take someone with little or no knowledge of the plan and teach and mentor them to be great leaders who are willing to carry on the mission even after he is gone.

I touched the mantle of my faith to let all the people who have lost faith in the church know that there is still a spiritual remnant of the "Church of Antioch" functioning on the earth that is accepting of you right where you are and knows that being transformed and renewed in your hearts and minds is a process of healing, deliverance, and forgiveness in order to break the bondage that held us captive for so long. For me, the battle has begun for the hearts and minds of our young people. As a fifty-one-year-old, I'm writing this to reiterate that each generation has been in bondage and enslaved by too many supernatural things. I can say that the battle still wages on for me as well when someone asks me, "Who is your covering?" or "What denomination are you?" It is my choice to continue to uplift the Savior, lean on the teachings of Jesus, submit to the guidance of the Holy Spirit, and ultimately trust in God for all things.

Now, the Holy Spirit uses me and my wife to evangelize through our testimonies of praise to tell those that are hurting God still desires a personal relationship with them. Also, we let them know that we have walked in those same "church hurt" shoes and even to this day are not welcome in most churches because we don't have a "man-made covering." But if you think about it for a minute, neither did the apostles. They had Jesus and the Holy Spirit. And if that was good enough for them, I am believing in all faith that it will be good enough for us too. But we still desire to have that true fellowship of believers that will uplift, encourage, strengthen, and, more importantly, have a heart for us and our gifts.

God wants each of us to be the Joshuas and the Esthers of our generations who are willing to fight with Him in the spirit of truth and righteousness. When the army of wickedness and deception comes to us as a flood, He commands that we hold up that spiritual standard before, during, and after the spiritual battle. This battle is for the minds and souls of men. God doesn't need our land, cars, or personal property because He has already given it to us. God doesn't give us titles; we are all servants underneath Him because He created all things. Believers of Christ should not want to be served because Christ didn't come to be served but to serve. So, we must understand that the *battle* of our warfare is not natural but spiritual. This *battle* has become more prevalent and very evident today to divide and destroy the teachings of Jesus Christ.

The Bible tells us in John 4:24 (NKJV), "God *is* Spirit, and those who worship Him must worship in spirit and truth." If we are worshiping with a truthful heart and mind, why should we be restricted to a certain protocol? In "spirit" means that we are connecting to Christ without bodily restrictions or emotional restraints. This can only be done by laying aside every weighted sin or connected bondage that tries to restrict us from experiencing the glorious freedom and peace that God has for us in our worship.

Once a person repents, seeks forgiveness from the Lord, and turns from their wicked ways, Christ will heal them and purge their hearts from the bondage of sin. Christ's blood will become smeared on the heart and mind of the new believer so that sin is conquered within them. Christ is the bondage breaker, and the Holy Spirit seals the wounds and scars that are left behind once a person is delivered. Jesus breaks the chains of low self-esteem and emotional depression because He told us that if we believe in Him, we will hunger and thirst no more for the acceptance of His love. Christ told us with His own words, "You are the light of the world" (Matthew 5:14; NKJV). We are so rich in kindness and radiance that we cannot be hidden or held in bondage any more.

Christ wants us to reveal the light of love and patience when we are delivered from all bondage so that we can show others how to allow Christ to break the chains that held them in bondage. Bondage is a spiritual attack that happens to everyone, but Christ is the answer. He desires to be accepted into our hearts and minds to deliver and break the chains of bondage that may control or restrict us from fully giving our hearts to Him. In order for any bondage and sin to release us, we must bring it under the authority of the Son of "the Most High God" (Mark 5:7; NKJV). There has to be a total regression of self and complete surrender to Christ's authority so that Jesus can claim authority over that evil to expel it from your life.

After that, the Holy Spirit is sent to infill and seal those broken and oppressed places in our mind, body, and soul, with peace, love, grace, truth, and mercy. What the devil once held captive; only Christ can heal, deliver, and set free. Christ affirmed to us that He will never leave us or forsake us; we have also read that He will supply all our needs according to His riches in glory. So, there is no need for us to sell our souls to the devil for bread because Christ is the bread of life or to enslave ourselves to spiritual bondage because He wants us to "*Let* love *be* without hypocrisy. Abhor [hate] what is evil. Cling to what is good."(Romans 12:9; NKJV).

If you've been hurt by people in the church or by someone in the body of Christ, please know that it was not Christ and that all men are flawed with self-will. No matter how much they try to restrain from their sinful nature, it sometimes returns. But if we learn to look beyond the faults of the messenger and hear the true message, then we can forgive those who have hurt us or held us in bondage and continue to proclaim the works of Christ. Our mess can be our message, and our test will be our testimony. Finally, when we let go and submit ourselves to the Holy Spirit, He will then, take control of our hearts and renew our thoughts; ultimately, we will become a blessed part of the true church that Christ will build for others to see and witness.

FAITH

"Grace, the Blood & His Blessings"

I know that you don't understand how infinite my Grace is
I paid a ransom price
There's nothing that can change it, no matter what you've done
I have already forgiven you, Learn to love yourself and others
Seek the truth and walk in humility
Allow me to reveal my glory as you feel my sunlight
I am healing your soul through the prayers you prayed
When it rains I replenish your needs with each raindrop that I send
Listen to the birds as they sing
I have the power to fulfill, my spirit moves when you believe
Let no one deter you
If you walk with me I will teach you as you grow
There's nothing that I will withhold if you surrender
I will purge your iniquities then open the windows of
heaven to you

Speak to My Heart, Lord

"But the Lord said to Samuel, "Do not look at his appearance or at his physical stature, because I have refused him. For *the Lord does* not *see* as man sees; for man looks at the outward appearance, but the Lord looks at the heart." (1 Samuel 16:7 NKJV)

"If you declare with your mouth, 'Jesus is Lord,' and believe in your heart that God raised him from the dead, you will be saved. For it is with your heart that you believe and are justified, and it is with your mouth that you profess your faith and are saved." (Romans 10:9–10; NIV)

Yes, worship! There are so many scripture readings in the Bible and other books that clearly affirms that mankind was created by God for the purpose of worship. God desires that we worship Him supernaturally and honestly. Also, we must come to God in reverence, fear, and submission to His presence; this may be difficult if a person has never exhibited these types of feelings in their lives. Please understand that Jesus is Lord and at His name, every knee will bow and every tongue will confess that He is Lord. Additionally, God is almighty, sovereign, just, truth, and our Creator.

When Jesus started His ministry, He began in humility and reverence to the mission that God ordained Him to accept as His role before man was created. He understood the ramifications that were already planned for Him and still embraced His destiny. Jesus said, "not My will, but Yours, be done" (Luke 22:42; NKJV).We must be willing to give ourselves in total surrender to God when we know that we are in His presence and are under the divine authority of God. This is important when we worship Him as servants. Even the Son of God knew that God is "I AM" and that there must be total obedience and reverence to God's purpose and will. Many of us forget our true calling and revert back to the world by believing that we need to be worshipped and held in great honor due to our titles or positions; however, just like the rich man in the Bible who Jesus explained to him and those around Him, that we "cannot serve God and mammon" (Matthew 6:24; NKJV).

Consequently, some of us believe that money has given us the authority to act as gods. We work hard all our adult lives to attain a certain position at a job or social elevation which causes another person or peer to hold us in the highest regard because of our accomplishments. Therefore, we begin to feel the prideful power and authority of being higher than or greater than others who have less.

People with prideful hearts become inflamed with pride, vanity, and conceit as the visual prestige begin to take root. Let us be mindful by reading in the Bible (Daniel 4) about a king named Nebuchadnezzar, who believed that he built and sustained all the riches and power that he gazed upon and pridefully spoke about without God's blessings. He was warned to give thanks and worship God with thanksgiving, yet he failed to heed the warning. God often sends us warnings and signs when we are headed down a path that is displeasing to Him. We cannot be so entangled in what we see with our physical eyes that we lose sight of the love and unmerited favor of God over our total lives. This means our worship and praise must be all about God. Our praise must be filled with exaltations of gracious praise. Going back to the King Nebuchadnezzar, he paid a price for pride; the king was stripped of his dignity and position because of his arrogance and pride. God's punishment was noticeable and resolute. God took him out of the perfect situation that he had and thrust him into an unknown and totally humiliating situation where he took on the mannerism of a wild beast. He ate and walked on all fours, his fingernails grew as claws, and he ate from the ground.

This was all because of pride. We must remain receptive to God's love because it is God who gives us wealth and made the heavens and the earth. He has all the riches and grace that we would ever need, and all that He desires from us is that we worship Him supernaturally without restraint and truthfully with everything within us. Our thanks and worship to God connects us to remain humbled and grateful for the blessings and supernatural covering over our lives, so that we can become living witnesses of God's sustaining power of provision, prosperity, and purpose.

The results of King Nebuchadnezzar's prideful thinking, ensured that God had to humble him by confusing his thoughts and mind to thinking he was wild and untamed (Daniel 4). Thus, prideful thinking and an overzealous mannerism is sinful and this leads a person to believe that they are more than everyone and no longer need the blessings of the Creator to lead and guide them. When a person is so boastful and prideful, they believe that they are equal to God and God's first commandment is now broken as it tells us in Exodus 20:3–5 (NKJV), "You shall have no other gods before me. You shall not make for yourself a carved image—any likeness *of anything* that is in heaven above, or that *is* in the earth beneath, or that *is* in the water under the earth; you shall not bow down to them or serve them. For I, the Lord your God, *am* a jealous God, visiting the iniquity of the fathers upon the children to the third and the fourth *generations* of those who hate Me," and if this commandment is broken, you have sinned, and "the wages of sin *is* death" (Romans 6:23; NKJV). However, you can change the death sentence. You can reverse the curse and eliminate the distractions that push you away from God's love and peace.

Our hearts and minds must be receptive to allow the Lord to speak to us. More importantly, we must repent and ask the Lord to speak to our hearts and to reveal His love and grace to us so that we won't forget what it feels like when we are going through our tests and trials. In spite of our natural situations, God's requirements are still the same. He looks at our hearts, and our hearts are what will allow us to accept the gift of salvation because it is the heart that holds the supernatural connection to Christ. It is by grace through faith that we are saved, it is with our hearts that we give God perfected praise, and, lastly, it is within our hearts that Christ destroys the bondage of pride, envy, jealousy, and overall sin.

The Bible continues to tell us about a king named Josiah (2 Chronicles 34), who repented with anguish and deep sorrow after learning that his people were facing God's wrath for not worshipping the Creator with their whole hearts. But He didn't stop at repentance; Josiah started to take action by cleansing the temples, hearts, and minds of his people. They began to ask God to forgive and speak to their hearts so that they would no longer sin against Him.

God wants us to do just as King Josiah when we know that we are out of fellowship with Him. He wants us to ask Him, "Speak to my heart, Lord"; the only way that God will speak to you is when your heart has been cleansed (Psalm 51) and you are ready to worship Him in spirit and in truth. Jesus loved us so much that He became the intercessor and the advocate for us when our hearts were still clouded with sin and evil. He petitioned to God to give us more time to connect our hearts back to Him. Have you asked God to speak to your heart today? Have you cleared a path through repentance, obedience, and reverence in your heart so that God can renew it?

It starts with your worship and honesty. Josiah saw the state of his people and immediately repented and changed the path of his people to end their sin and remember the God of their fathers, the "I AM."

Many people are very protective of their hearts when it comes to building relationships. I can recall being very protective of my heart and emotions after I divorced. I was guarded and resigned not to show my feelings to anyone. This was mainly due to me developing an attitude of not trusting women anymore. This behavior soon bled over into other relationships as well. I started to be more guarded and detached from the soldiers and men that I served in the army with as well, even though I knew it wasn't their fault. I was hurting and emotionally devastated, but the feelings of love, loyalty, support, and trust were still there; I just had a horrible time trying to connect with those emotions at that time.

My emotional state of mind became my idol, meaning all my time was spent harboring the bad feelings and insecurities from a failed marriage, and this caused all other relationships to suffer. My heart was no longer open to loving or being loved. All that I thought about was the pain and the anxiety I was feeling. I easily incorporated all those feelings with drinking; I was an emotional time bomb that no one wanted to be around when it finally went off. Just like the children of Israel, I knew God was there, but the energy I put into feeding my shame, guilt, and emotions kept me away from His grace, love, and mercy. My heart was occupied with what I now understand to be "distractions." Could this be similar to an idol or god that has your heart now?

These distractions came hard and heavy in my life. The devil often came to me after the fifth drink of whiskey and reminded me of my shortcomings and failures because he is the real "accuser of the brethren" and he played that role very well. He would tell me that I wasn't good enough, so I started buying material things to make me look good. He told me that I wasn't attractive, so I started to try to emulate someone out of a magazine. He even told me that I wasn't good enough to be a father and husband to anyone, and I felt that I couldn't argue with that, so the devil had me believing that I was no longer good enough for God because I had been divorced not once but three times! He told me that I was a failure because my children had struggled and grew up faster than they should have. I agreed and sulked in disdainful shame by eventually passing out in the floor.

I can recall feeling that there was nothing worse than feeling that the natural and supernatural worlds were disappointed in me. I continued to suffer in silence by listening to the old dragon tell me constantly, "This is happening to you because God doesn't love you" and "You can't keep a good marriage because God hates you." My favorite lie was when he told me, "You can't be happy because your father never loved you." My heart sank deeper and deeper into shame and hurt.

Unfortunately, I really started to believe every one of Satan's fiery darts. So, I lashed out with fury! I started trying to turn my loved ones away from me through anger; I would purposely stop communication with my children because I wanted them to find a better representative for a father. My heart had grown very cold and distant toward women who may have been interested, but most of all, I forgot God. I lost communication with and connection to Him. My beating red heart was a dark and hurting place of multiple cold, black clouds. I existed like this for three years. I was going through daily life drinking, going to work drinking, trying to date drinking, talking and interacting drinking.

It wasn't until one day when I was completely overwhelmed with my life as a single parent of four with three grandkids, no money, eviction notices, shut off notices, and illness that I was at the end. The devil had me completely crushed as a person and as a man. Then, faintly, I could hear a worship song being sung by Carlton Pearson called, "Father I stretch my hand to thee." I cried out to God to help me. I called on the name of Jesus. I was severely depressed, totally broken and contritely deep in my existence. I love each of the verses that are outlined in the beginning of this chapter, not for the profoundness but for the simplicity in the message that each scripture gives us. As God began to break the emotional bondage and the chains of spiritual brokenness, He helped me look back at my life to a time of pain and remorse. I began to understand that when I was growing up as a teenager, I often felt a sense of loneliness and disconnection from my environment. This, I now believe, was due to the separation and distance that I experienced between my father and me. I truly wanted and needed my father's acceptance and respect when I became a young father and parent.

I can truly say that it was hard to understand what people were requiring of me, meaning I didn't have the common sense that others had. I needed that fatherly advice to help me to stand strong, be the man of my house, and never give up my position in my home. Also, I needed my father to provide me with mature wisdom in dealing with situations, finances, problems, and my own insecurities. That fatherly connection is priceless because we have a chance to pour out our hearts as men to each other, asking the "hard," sacred questions that men ask each other about love, women, sex, life, and finances. This wasn't there for me, and as a result, I hid naivety and ignorance in my heart by masking my insecurities with an outward appearance of having it all together.

I often hear people say, "Primal nature teaches us that only the strong survive"; I wasn't strong. I was hurting, lost, alone, and afraid. My heart was filled with anger, disappointment, hurt, and fear. There was no real room for anything positive to grow and manifest positivity. I needed and longed for my fatherly approval but never received it. He died, and I never heard the words, "Son, I'm proud of you," "I love you son," or "You've done a great job with your family." Each of these statements that so many people take for granted were never given to me and were never spoken to me by my father. I was a parent with four children looking to me for guidance and help; they respected me as a father, a parent, and the head of the household, yet I was still harboring the ills of my childhood, my disappointments, my hurt, and my anger in my heart. This made it hard to receive love because I wasn't able to fully give love. But God! He continued to shield me from myself.

I am reminded of the story in the Bible regarding Balaam and his donkey (Numbers 22:1–39; NIV). Balaam was riding his donkey on the road, believing that all was well and he was safe. Everything looked right as all other times, but that was not true. There was an angel of the Lord standing in the path waiting for Balaam to reach him so that he could slay Balaam for recklessness and sin against God. But God opened the donkey's eyes while approaching the angel to see what was about to happen; the donkey stopped and refused to go forward. This angered Balaam so much He started beating the donkey, and the angel had to reveal to Balaam that if it had not been for the faithful donkey, he would have been destroyed. The angel told Balaam, "I have come here to oppose you because your path is a reckless one before me." God sent so many warnings and people into my life to help me to release the anger and pain. I started buying gospel CDs and sermons in the hope that they would crack the feelings of pain and anger, but I didn't pay attention. I was just as angry as Balaam beating on the faithful donkey. I could not find my purpose or balance in life because my life was no longer mine—it belonged to my pain.

I was a living example that hurt people hurt people. By this time, I didn't know how to turn off the pain or the anger. I wandered in this hopeless "wilderness" state for sixteen years. My heart was so far from love and life. So, I self-medicated with liquor, women, and empty relationships. It wasn't until a very nice person in my life, Denise, told me best that all she saw surrounding me was a dark cloud.

"Dark cloud?" That really stopped me in my tracks because I thought that I had hidden my heart and emotions from everyone, even

God! But that was not the case. The Lord told Samuel that man sees the outward appearances of man, but He sees our hearts. This was the wakeup call I needed for God to speak to my heart. I needed to be shaken up and fixed, but I did not know how to make contact with the Lord. I felt so alone and lonely. I was so afraid, afraid that my life would eventually come to a meaningless end. The fear of knowing that you are going to hell completely overwhelms the fear of being alone on earth. I didn't want to die and go to hell for my sinful ways and my unrepentant heart. I can remember one night feeling a sense of hopeless and depravity so great that I began to cry and lift up my heart to the Lord. I began to really have a talk with God.

"Lord, I am so angry! At everything! Why is everything so completely messed up? I'm angry and hurting, and I don't know where to place all of this anger. My father is gone, so I can't tell him how I'm feeling. My mother, my sisters, my children—none of them will understand the pain and suffering that I'm feeling! help Me, God!"

As I lay down broken, in tears, and personally destroyed, I could hear a faint whisper in my ear telling me, "Go get Bishop G. E. Patterson's CD *Singing the Old Time Way*, and play it." I searched my collection, finally found the CD, and started to play it as I nestled in the bed. Bishop Patterson started to tell the story from Mark 5 as he expounded about a man who had been possessed by a legion of unclean spirits. For some reason, my ears started to only focus on the words from this CD. As Bishop Patterson continued to tell the story, I could feel the spiritual connection in my soul connecting to every word he was professing through the CD.

He began to sing a song called "Jesus Breaks Every Fetter," Immediately, I could somehow see the words being played out as a movie in my head visually! I could see the man lying there as Jesus commanded the unclean sprits to come out of this man! I saw me, and I saw Christ telling me, "I love you, I can take your pain, and I can set you free from your bondage. Worship Me! Love Me! Because

I love you in your brokenness! I'm here." I immediately felt the words of Jesus commanding the anger, sin, depravity, and hopelessness to come out of me! And at that moment, I wept—I wept so hard that I woke up from my sleep, crying and saying, "Thank You, Jesus!" Deep in my heart, I could feel the burden of carrying the hurt, anger, and insecurity in my heart. I laid there in bed, giving God thanks and telling Jesus, "Yes, Lord. Thank You for Your healing power over my life."

The next day, I felt so much lighter in my spirit. I had never felt this peaceful in my life. I wanted to bathe in this feeling, hold on to this uplifting feeling, but I wasn't sure how. I grabbed my Bible—since Bishop sang about a story in the Bible, I can find more in it—and opened it. What was so miraculous about this time is as I flipped open the Bible, it opened to Psalm 51:10 (NKJV), which reads, "Create in me a clean heart, O God, and renew a right spirit within me." That was ten years ago, and since that time, I have continually petitioned to the Lord to speak to my heart and continue to fill me with the Holy Spirit. I am always cautious not to allow thoughts and feelings to enter into my heart and soul. I leave it up to the Holy Spirit to release them from me.

In order to appreciate the magnitude of this blessing, you have to understand what type of person I became. I now realize that my "concentric circle" was flawed. A concentric circle is a mathematical term in which two or more circles have the same center point, and when we think of how a concentric circle relates to our lives, we can envision each of the relationships that we have as a circle. We label each circle as a sustained relationship, such as spiritual, family, social, and extended people we know, with one common factor in their lives: you. I tried desperately to hold on to the biblical teachings of my childhood to find the balance and strength to raise my children.

However, without fully releasing my father from the pain and anger that I felt toward him, I was restricted from giving my children all the love and strength they needed from me. If you saw my outward appearance, you would have thought that I had all my "ducks in a row." But deep in my heart, I was still trying to figure out what was required and needed of me from my children. I began to do as I had done for so many years: I made it up as I went forth. And boy, did I mess things up.

We are sometimes thrown into unchartered situations and circumstances that hurt us to the fabric of our hearts, causing us to change the direction of our lives. Many people that survived devastation and emotional, debilitating turmoil mask the pain and resort to an alternative way of existing because it is easier to mask and shelve the hurt and pain than to fight through the devastation.

Sometimes, we are like this as believers in Christ: our hearts are so engulfed with the hurt, pain, and agony that we suffered while living in our circumstances that we never give our spiritual Father the opportunity to mend our brokenness, or we prevent access to speak to our hearts deeply enough to release the spiritual bondage that we hold on to and carry from natural relationships to supernatural relationships. This cycle of hurt keeps revolving in every relationship, yielding the same results. I truly thank God for His mercy and grace!

I have learned that through most valleys, there is a river of water that comes down from the mountain top to help sustain life to those in the valley. Christ is that river for many of us who are in our valley of despair or trauma. He is the emotional healer that can restore your joy. He is the Redeemer who paid the price for all the pain and suffering that you have endured when He suffered so profoundly on the way to be crucified. The Bible gives us a written analogy of Christ's love and missional purpose for everyone that has survived domestic violence, rape, emotional abuse, physical abuse, incarcerations, bullying, and separation. In Isaiah 53:5 (NKJV), there is an explanation of Christ's message for accepting our pain and suffering: "But He *was* wounded for our transgressions, *He was* bruised for our iniquities; the chastisement for our peace *was* upon Him, and by His stripes we are healed."

We are healed from our past pain. We are healed from the domestic violence that plagued us for years as we mask the suffering while still broken and beaten by what we thought was inseparable love. We are healed from the horror of being raped and stripped of all dignity that comes from someone forcing and taking your soul and heart from you. You are healed from believing that you were created for pain and suffering.

Sons and daughters, you were created because God loves you so much that He wants your worship. Your worship is special to Him, and your testimony of being an overcomer through the pain reveals who you were and who you are. By internalizing the suffering of the Redeemer of all pain and sin, we can finally let go of the hurt and pain knowing that Christ is our ultimate chastisement of peace on that day so long ago. We can now release our hearts knowing that we are healed, and we can let it all go in Jesus name.

"Speak to our hearts, Lord. Take away the pain, take the suffering from our minds, and release the guilt that we feel when we are led to believe that we must have done something to cause the pain and suffering that we endured. Renew the right spirit within us that gives us inner peace, and restore to us the joy and love that we were created to have in our lives. We are broken, we need help, and we reach out to You for divine love, spiritual restoration, and a supernatural healing to be called back to worship You with our entire mended hearts. This we ask and believe in Jesus's name."

In the Bible, there was a king of Israel named David who was chosen by God to lead the nation of Israel during the Iron Age II (1010–970 BC). King David was broken and hurting when he realized he had done many things against God's will and plan for his life. However, God, His Spiritual Father, let everyone know that He had a heart for David and that He was pleased with him as king of the chosen nation of Israel. Yet in spite of knowing this, David still sinned against God. Man saw the outside disappointment and actions that

David committed, but God saw David's heart. You see, our hearts are required of God, and our hearts cannot be presented to the sovereign God until they are purified, renewed, and healed.

Now, I petition to the Lord Jesus to keep standing as my protector from those unclean spirits and to cast them away from me. I pray that the Lord will speak to my heart and repair the wounds that the enemy has tried to reopen and upend into my life daily. Have you asked Christ to renew and speak to your heart? Have you been battling and struggling with something that you can't seem to break free from? The Bible tells us that we can cast all our cares on Christ because He cares for us. All it takes is a repentant heart that wants to hear Christ's voice. Do not harden your heart (Hebrews 3:15). It is God's will that none of us should perish but come to repentance. Deliverance is a process that demands commitment and faith. Deliverance is an event that releases a person from the natural struggles and strongholds that have them bound and plagued with depravity and hopelessness that can totally control and stifle their understanding of who God is and why Jesus loves them so much that He sacrificed His life so that you (the person dealing with something that you are ashamed of) can be set free and delivered from the hands of their bondage.

When we experience the voice and supernatural presence of Christ through the Holy Spirit, we become newly created people who are delivered from the fetters of sin and immorality to be reborn into a new creature that loves the Lord and loves life. When we accept Christ into our hearts and minds, we are then transformed and renewed with the active fruit of the Spirit that nourishes our hearts with peace and joy, overflowing to the point that we cannot contain the feelings of being born again. Becoming born again in Christ Jesus exhibits in our lives the total surrendering of ourselves so that we can live, move, and have our being that resembles the fruit of the Spirit, which "is love, joy, peace, longsuffering, kindness, goodness, faithfulness, gentleness, self-control" (Galatians 5:22–23; NKJV). And after all these things, know that His power will rest, rule, and abide within you because *you* have filled those cracks and dents in your heart with the Spirit of Christ. Now we must stand and believe that Christ can do abundantly and exceedingly everything that we can ask of Him for our lives. This includes healing, delivering, and setting us free through our worship.

I pray that Christ remains my advocate and Redeemer and that He will strengthen us as we continue to be the clay pots He is continually shaping to be mighty witnesses of God.

CHAPTER SEVEN

God, Give Me Strength

"For God has not given us a spirit of fear, but of power and of love and of a sound mind." (2 Timothy 1:7; NKJV) "I can do all things through Christ who strengthens me." (Philippians 4:13; NKJV) "Yet in all these things we are more than conquerors through Him who loved us." (Romans 8:37; NKJV)

No matter what we come up against in our walk with the Lord, we have to always have faith knowing that the Lord is there and He will never leave us nor forsake us. Even when times start to get hard and situations overtake us, we have to remain confident knowing that nothing can harm us or steal the joy and peace that we have in Christ. This was my understanding after rededicating my life and heart back to Christ. I was free; I was a new creature that knew my Creator. God loves me and has a purpose for my life. Now, you have to understand that it was my extreme, both emotionally and physically and I had completely lost my way. I had to realize the fact that I was emotionally broken. This caused me to submit to the truth I needed the Holy Spirit to indwell my life and that I had to rely on the Holy Spirit to give me strength to stay connected to the Lord.

You see, the enemy heard my cries of uncontrolled repentance and my submission back unto the holiness of God. I felt as if he had lost something and needed to "reclaim me." I'm here to tell each of you that God does not give us the spirit of fear but of power, love, and a sound mind, so stand on the Word of God where it tells us to prepare ourselves by transforming our hearts and minds unto the authority of Christ and live in the blessed assurance that He is the King of kings and Lord of lords in our lives. Once you give all of your pain and struggles to the Lord on the altar of forgiveness, then you can confidently answer this question, "Is there anything too hard for God?"

Jeremiah 32:17 (NKJV) tells us with conviction and confidence, "Ah, Lord God! Behold, You have made the heavens and the earth by Your great power and outstretched arm. There is nothing too hard for you." Jeremiah needed strength to complete the mission that God had instructed him to do in the midst of the exile of the Israelites. This is very similar to what is required of us. We will be persecuted and talked about for our belief in Christ. We will be talked about for the uniqueness of our calling just like Jeremiah. But we have to know that there is nothing too hard for God. Consequently, if He sanctioned you to do as He commands, it is you who must obey and follow the voice of the Lord.

Every heartfelt believer has a unique purpose in life to draw those that are lost and hurting to the healing center, which is in Christ, to be healed, delivered, and set free. Just like Jeremiah and other major and minor prophets in the Old Testament, their strength was reinforced through their obedience, allowing each of them to complete the calling on their lives. Please know that each one of them called on God to give them strength, to protect them, and to reassure them that He was still there.

That's why it's important to understand the scripture (Matthew 22:14; NKJV) that "many are called, but few *are* chosen." You have to hear and connect with the voice of the Lord in all kingdom tasks in order for your journey to be effective in tearing down strongholds. Today, we can be assured that there are a lot of people who have been called by God to live for Him and to serve Him in spirit and in truth. They are given unmerited favor (grace) to live a life that pleases God and to be a testimony of mercy. There is a measure of strength that each of us as believers must believe the Lord for. Jesus told us in Acts to wait for the promise, and that promise is "power" after the baptism of the Holy Ghost. Then, we shall be witnesses of Him to the entire world.

So, our power and strength reside in our submission and infilling of the Holy Spirit. The Holy Spirit gives each believer the power to war in the supernatural according to scripture. Christ has given us supernatural strength to cast out demons in His name. God also made us a little lower than the angels, but we have been disconnected from our holy power by sin, thus robbing us of God's strength to trample over disillusions, mysticism, witchcraft, and demonic encouragement. We cannot be effective if we are fearful of the journey. We must embrace everything that God has ordained us to complete or endure with commitment and courage to know that He is with us. We must know that we are chosen to accomplish the work that has been given to us.

It doesn't matter if others do not understand the exact nature of your calling or mission; what matters is that you complete the work and mission that was given to you. So, as we look back into the history books and Christian literature, many leaders that were called by God to lead or correct the children of Israel were not popular people or men and women of stature; however, God was able to see their hearts and know that they were internally able to be obedient and humble enough to allow God to lead them. It is with this principle that we gain strength to complete the calling on our lives.

Lastly, God gives us strength when we encounter natural disappointments that seem too hard to overcome, but Peter told us, "Cast all your anxiety on him for he cares for you" (1 Peter 5:7; NIV). So, don't be afraid of your belief or your faith. Don't you know that you serve a God who has been tested and tried throughout the ages against the pagan gods and mystical beings that were created by men only to reveal that He is the Almighty and the Creator of all things old and new? Your strength resides in your faith.

Faith gives us the ability to believe and receive. Our faith allows us to walk through situations in our lives when we cannot see the outcome. By faith, we know that Christ is ruler of all and that God did not give us the spirit of fear when we can't see the whole picture. If you are encountering darkness and pain, turn to Christ and look to Him for help and inner peace, for He has peace and joy in abundance for those who accept Him as Lord over their lives.

Please understand me when I say that our faith is all about Christ. Christ is who drives Christianity. Christ is who empowers the believers. Christ is who redeems. Christ is who saves. Christ is who heals, delivers, and sets free those that are captive. For me, I understood that the ministry of Jesus Christ is founded in love, repentance, faith, compassion, truth, and obedience. Jesus showed love and grace to those that came to Him for help and healing. Jesus was able to love those that were considered castaways and forsaken. The Bible illustrates in Luke 17:11–19 (NKJV) how Jesus went into a certain village where He met ten lepers that were not permitted to come into the village. They were exiled from the community and shunned from society because of their situation. The lepers were still human beings, yet they were labeled and thrown aside to deal with their problems by themselves. Have you ever felt that your community or "concentric circle" of friends have often abandoned you when situations or illness came upon you? Do you feel that you have been branded in some sort of way as a "leper" or a sinful nobody that should be ashamed because of what you are going through or have endured? It's interesting that our circle of friends sometimes forget the good and always remember the bad. But Jesus heard the ten men from afar off, lifting their voices and saying, "Jesus, Master, have mercy on us!" (Luke 17:13; NKJV).

The Bible continues to tell us "He saw them" (Luke 17:14; NKJV), meaning Jesus saw that they pressed their way by faith, and they believed so greatly that they were willing to have faith enough to see Jesus no matter the consequences. They believed that Jesus was the mercy seat they needed to heal them. If we define the word *mercy*, we find that it means forgiveness and kindness; in Latin, it means "price paid wages." The ten lepers were looking for mercy and forgiveness from their situation. They did not ask for the leprosy sickness; it wasn't something they did to deserve the horrible affliction, yet it became theirs, and the people around them made sure that they owned it.

Today, many of us may be in situations that we did not ask for, yet some of our peers or people will not have mercy on us in our situations or socially forgive us for the wrongs that we may have committed. Consequently, we are branded and treated like lepers because we may have "backslid" or lost faith and committed a sin. When we are branded by our peers as "lepers," there is a stigma among those that know us that we are no longer worthy to be in their company or even to fellowship with them. This can be devastating to the person whom the Bible affirmed that we are all sinners "saved by grace" and that forgiveness is paramount for our spiritual growth. Now is the time to believe that God's grace is sufficient. Paul taught on many occasions that we are to live a life that reveals love, kindness, joy, peace, and goodness. Also, he reiterates in Galatians 6:2 (NKJV), "Bear one another's burdens, and so fulfill the law of Christ."

Paul wanted the Galatian church to understand that we are knitted together in love and grace. Believers should not have a problem coming to the aid of anyone who needs help because of the law of Christ. Also, the law of Christ, found in Mark 12:32–33, tells us that loving God and our neighbor is the greatest of all commandments; it is even greater than any offering or sacrifice of monetary or natural value that we as individuals can give.

Sometimes, it is our "community of believers" who denies "mercy" or "kindness" to us as they start to forget that "There is none righteous, no, not one" (Romans 3:10; NKJV). Christ knew all too well about forgiveness and mercy because He is clothed in mercy and righteousness and drenched with forgiveness. He taught that "For if you forgive men their trespasses, your heavenly Father will also forgive you. 15 But if you do not forgive men their trespasses, neither will your Father forgive your trespasses." (Matthew 6:14-15 NKJV). Although we know that society no longer suffers from leprosy; but, the spirit of "leprosy" (unforgiveness and persecution) is still rampant among us today. Jesus was even asked by one of His disciples, Peter, "'Lord, how often will my brother sin against me, and I forgive him? As many as seven times?' Jesus said to him, 'I do not say to you seven times, but seventy times seven'" (Matthew 18:21–22; ESV). The lepers may have asked for forgiveness from the village people and wanted to be welcomed back into their homes; they may have wanted to be treated by the town physician for illnesses as well. Maybe the lepers even wanted to feel compassion and love in spite of their infirmities, but no one showed love and compassion toward them. Instead, they were made to feel ashamed and less than human for their sickness.

Sin is a sickness that attacks our minds to make us believe that we are supposed to be cast aside or that we are supposed to live in sin, but that is not the case! God told us in Isaiah 43:25–26 (NIV) that "I, even I, am he who blots out your transgressions, for my own sake, and remembers your sins no more. Review the past for me, let us argue the matter together; state the case for your innocence."

During this time, some of the townspeople may have argued that they themselves were living lives that did not cause "those" afflictions to come upon them, so they were better or more blessed than the lepers. You can make that argument, but can anyone honestly say that they have not broken ANY of these laws (past or present) in the following list? Do not embarrass others; do not oppress the weak;

do not speak derogatorily of others; do not take revenge; do not bear a grudge; do not follow the whims of your heart or what your eyes see; do not inquire of spirits; do not consult magicians or seers; do not be superstitious; do not engage in astrology; do not go into a trance to foresee events, etc.; do not tattoo the skin; men must not wear women's clothing; women must not wear men's clothing; do not walk outside the city boundary on the Sabbath; do not wear cloth woven of wool and linen. These are only sixteen of the 613 laws and/ or commandments that are written in the Old Testament scriptures that the children of Israel were required to live by.

Thank God that, by grace through faith, we found redemption and became the living miracles of grace and salvation by understanding that it will take more than the laws to convert our thoughts. Each of the laws was written to prepare our hearts and minds for the salvation of the Messiah that was promised in Isaiah 7:14 and Isaiah 61:1–2. This message is still important today. Romans 3:23 (NIV) tells us "for all have sinned and fall short of the glory of God." It's good to know that we can still live as close to holiness by the laws and commandments as humanly possible, but it is only by being transformed and renewed in our minds and hearts and living justified by faith that helps us to understand that everyone needs help and mercy at some point in our lives.

So, it is apparent that God and His Son, Jesus, do extend mercy! The same mercy that the lepers lifted up their voices to Jesus for. We have to be willing to raise our expectations for forgiveness and mercy if we want to be truly delivered from something. We have to ask, seek, and knock with humility for God's mercy just as the lepers of the Bible. Rescue and salvation comes when we raise our expectations and voices for it. This is still very apropos to our walk with Christ today. Christ wants to heal our hearts and bodies from all the natural pains and hurt that we are encircled into. It's not hard to find Christ in our struggle; all we have to do is call on Him in our situational pain. We have to cry out to the Lord, "Lord, save me." Paul says it best that "whoever calls on the name of the Lord shall be saved" (Romans 10:13; NKJV).

This concludes all aspects of salvation or redemption and fulfills the prophetic discourse of Joel 2:32 (NKJV) that it will "come to pass *that* whoever calls on the name of the Lord shall be saved. For on Mount Zion and in Jerusalem there shall be deliverance, as the Lord has said, among the remnant whom the Lord calls." Are you the remnants that the Lord is calling to stand tall and be strong? Have you cried out to the Lord to give you strength? Are you seeking the Holy Spirit's guidance of love and compassion to help someone who has lost their spiritual way so that you can let them know that "God still loves them"? Have you prayed to the God of Abraham, Isaac, and Jacob for strength to be the messenger of the good news of Jesus Christ to the "lepers" in your community to help those who are still drenched in sin, depravity, supernatural bondage, and physical abuse? If not, let us ask the Holy Spirit to give us the anointed words to remove the shackles and to bind and remove the curse that plague our generations.

It takes the Holy Spirit to restore order and mercy by tearing down the strongholds that weaken our faith to believe that we are more than conquerors through Him that loved us. If Christ healed and delivered the ten leapers after they lifted their voices and if Christ is telling us to love and forgive others, shouldn't we listen and allow the Holy Spirit that rests, rules, and abides within us to share love and faith to everyone? We must plant the seeds of deliverance and faith so that salvation can draw near to those that want it. Also, if they are thirsting after righteousness, we must bring them to the water of replenishment so that their souls can be revived through the baptism of the Holy Spirit, and when this is completed, we have to let go and let God give the increase of mercy, grace, and love so that those who are looking and seeking help can experience that they have been restored. Healing happens to many people, in most people, in the physical sense of surviving a disease or illness. Healing can also be considered a supernatural manifestation of what we call grace.

Wholeness means a deeper commitment to God, a more constant awareness of the indwelling Christ. So every time you feel a special moment of grace (healing) in your life, look to Jesus and thank him for the healing, then, by faith, through grace, keep moving a little closer, and grow in your devotion to Him. Start removing the things of this world that hold you in physical and spiritual bondage, so that you can hear Him (Jesus) say "you are made whole."

PEACE

"Now You See Me"

Now can you see me?
After the darkness has cleared, and my true purpose has appeared.
Now can you see me?
After the raindrops flow like rivers of tears that helped
cleanse me from my emotional bondage and pain.
Now can you see me?
As my helpless state reverses to know that God is with me.
Now can you see me?
After I've dropped all of my cares to solely trust
in the savior to protect me from myself.
Now can you see me?
After asking God to create in me a clean heart
and renew a right spirit within me.
Now can you see me?
After I asked the precious Holy Spirit's Heart to
Rest, Rule, and Abide within my soul.
Now can you see me?
As a living testimony of Christ supernatural
love and all-consuming Grace.
Now can you see me?
As the residual of a true living miracle of compassion,
commitment, and completion; this completion only
happened after the acceptance of Christ as Lord, and

a total submission to the power of the Holy Spirit that
continually rest, rule, and abides with me to bring peace.
Now do you see?
That there is no greater love, grace, and peace than
to be healed, delivered and set free; knowing that
God's power rest, rules, and abides within you.

Thomas E. Walker; Reflections of Grace Outreach Ministries

CHAPTER EIGHT

Love Lifted Me

"For God so loved the world that He gave His only begotten Son, that whoever believes in Him should not perish but have everlasting life." (John 3:16; NKJV)"Greater love has no one than this, than to lay down one's life for his friends." (John 15:13; NKJV) "But the fruit of the Spirit is love, joy, peace, long-suffering, kindness, goodness, faithfulness, [23] gentleness, self-control. Against such there is no law. " (Galatians 5:22–23; NKJV)

Sometimes we hear self-help evangelists propagate society with the superficial understanding that individuals can achieve greatness and fulfillment through their own motivational and instructional means. Also, people are told that greatness and peace can finally be obtained when they reach a certain pinnacle within their social status and intellect. This is partially correct because a person can be superficially happy with the wealth and prestige; they are able to live a life that allows them not to struggle with finances or encircle themselves with the social issues that the "less fortunate" may be experiencing. They are able to surround themselves with the appearances of having it all and enjoying life to the fullest.

However, deep down in their hearts, there may be feelings of complacency and loneliness. This often happens when they realize that the people around them are only out for what they can obtain from their riches. They realize that people are not always who they seem in their social circles, and frankly, some people really don't love you the way you may love them. God placed a set of moral laws to guide us while we are living on earth to help us to live holy, fulfilled, and loving lives. Most of these laws have become foundational in many societies today; these are called the Ten Commandments. Each commandment provides us with a basic understanding of God's love and expectation for us.

Can you recall the Ten Commandments? Here's a summary from Exodus 20:3–17 (NKJV):

1. You shall have no other gods before me.

2. You shall not make for yourself a carved image—any likeness *of anything* that *is* in heaven above, or that *is* in the earth beneath, or that *is* in the water under the earth.

3. You shall not take the name of the Lord your God in vain.

4. Remember the Sabbath day, to keep it holy.

5. Honor your father and your mother.

6. You shall not murder.

7. You shall not commit adultery.

8. You shall not steal.

9. You shall not bear false witness against your neighbor.

10. You shall not desire your neighbor's house … your neighbor's wife … nor anything that is your neighbor's.

He wanted us to experience what it is like for Him to supply all our needs and not work or worry about anything. Instead, through disobedience and freewill, man was exiled from the true presence of God's love and protection. Since then, we have been told that we must work, struggle, and become less than God's purpose and plan in order to live life because of the blatant disobedience of God's command to Adam, not Eve.

God loves us and wants to care and be there for us since He created us, but we get in the way of our own prosperity and salvation because we are always trying to use our "freewill" to fix things or rule situations in our lives. I am the first to understand that it is hard to remove self and let God lead our lives. It is difficult to allow God to prosper us in a way that adds no sorrow to it. We often become engulfed in living until we forget how to live. We begin to serve mammon (Matthew 6:24; NKJV) for direction and prosperity while forgetting that God is omnipotent and well able to provide for us. It has always been God's intention for us to live a sinless life free from the influences of mammon's and Jezebel's influences.

The Bible clearly tells us that if we "Trust in the LORD with all your heart, Do not depend on your own understanding; in all your ways remember him. Then he will make your paths smooth and straight" (Proverbs 3:5–6; NIRV). I continued to believe that I had "all the answers" and knew what was best for me. I even tried to work and obtain riches, power, prestige, and superficial respect from others only to see it crumble and disintegrate into dust.

I soon learned after my failures and obsessions that I needed a Savior to help me live a life without disappointment. It was God's intent for man to live in harmony through worship and fellowship in the beauty of holiness and also not to have a need for superficial things. He is more than willing to supply all our needs if we remain obedient and righteous before Him. I am now convinced that the only peace that has lasting effects in our lives is spiritual peace and spiritual direction through Christ. Although many may disagree with me on that conviction, I can personally say that I didn't truly feel peace in my natural life until I knew my spiritual purpose. God created every one of us with unique gifts and talents that separates us as individuals. We were also created to ultimately give honor and praise to our Creator with the talents and gifts that we're born with.

However, since we were born into the chaos of sin, each of us entered mankind through childbirth confused and separated from knowing the love of God. We began to worship and offer our gifts and talents to things and people that were not worthy of them. As the human race grew older, this caused an emotional and spiritual hunger for acceptance and gratitude.

I remember seeking the approval and acceptance from things that I could physically touch and sense; I sought after my mother's love, my siblings' love, people's love, and my children's love only to still feel hungry and needing more. I can also remember placing so many unnecessary burdens on my spouse to fulfill the hunger for love where I had been starved by others, but it wasn't fair to ask one person to fulfill the emotional or spiritual hunger for love that had been missing from any of my concentric circles. This is where I've always struggled because I wanted completion, acceptance, and love from people or things that did not have the capability to fulfill this in my life. So, I continued to struggle until I realized that it was even harder for me to give love completely because I was broken and empty. There was past baggage of loveless relationships and unfulfilled expectations in my life that plagued my present and disallowed me to give my heart or emotions to anyone or anything.

This feeling was similar to wandering in the wilderness at night in a sandstorm. I couldn't see or feel what I needed to survive because I was so shrouded in darkness, despair, and hopelessness. I needed and wanted love to embrace me and pull me from the darkness. I wanted to feel the warmth and security of the sunlight that we feel when we see glimmers of it on the distant horizon. I wanted to be set free from the past hurt and misunderstandings that held me captive in my present. I strongly desired redemption and salvation from my imprisonment.

Hopelessness is so easy to fall into but so hard to rise out of. Hopelessness drowns the mind and heart to believe that nothing and no one can save you and that nothing you do will be good enough for you to survive calamity. The desolation and feelings of despair enslave us and control our way of thinking and reacting. I can remember times when my emotions plagued me so deeply until they held me captive and confused. It was hard to come up with answers to help me provide for my family. It was even harder to find peace when I was so lost. Later in my life, I started to search for answers to why was my life so filled with confusion and emptiness. Why was my heart so confused and hardened toward others? Why did I feel so alone and helpless? As I look back, I realize that I was still morally broken (according to the Old Testament commandments), as well as still trying to find answers within myself, which caused me to prohibit God from showing me who I was and am in Him.

Many people go through life looking for the same answers to these questions only to give up and give in to the despair. With all the natural success and riches, they start to self-medicate with pride, vanity, drugs, alcohol, destructive relationships, and dangerous situations. There was a time that I believed it was easier to drink alcohol until I passed out than to turn to my Creator to fix things.

My life was unfulfilled at best. I was a failure in relationships, finances, and emotional situations until I became introverted and fell into a deep depression. I remained encircled in these feelings for four months. I was prescribed drugs which helped to correct the "physical imbalance," but they could not heal and take all the pain and feelings away, so I continued to look deep within myself with self-reflection and self-evaluation in hopes of finding that missing puzzle piece to my heart.

After constant thinking and drinking, the answer floated even further away. I had no idea or understanding what my next step would be. I was hoping that the end of my existence remained far away, but I wasn't even sure of that. Sometimes I would faintly remember certain Bible scriptures, distant murmurs of Sunday sermons that I had heard long ago, or talks that I had had with my old pastors. I would slightly hear a church song playing in my mind that sounded soothingly angelic and so anointed. It was in my extreme depravity as a man that God was trying to get my attention. I felt so disconnected from God. Where was He? How could I find Him? Why hadn't He saved me from this pain? I was so lost and didn't know what to do. The Bible tells us that God loves us and that it is not His will that any of us should perish but be allowed the opportunity for repentance (2 Peter 3:9; NKJV). I realized that I needed a spiritual balance that could solidify my physical imbalance.

But, how could I feel repentance? I was too busy wallowing in my emotion. I felt so distant from God. I knew that I had turned from Him, left him like a prodigal son, and run into my depravity with both eyes open. You see, I was raised knowing who God is and that His Son, Jesus Christ, died for my sins so that I may experience peace on earth as it is in heaven, yet I still ran—I still left His protection. This also made me realize that as a man, I might not be as forgiving or understanding as God.

A scripture came to my mind, telling me, "For God so loved the world that He gave His only begotten Son, that whoever believes in Him should not perish but have everlasting life" (John 3:16; NKJV). It's hard to climb out of depravity when we have lived so long in it, and it's hard to believe that there's hope when you've spent years living in despair. There is a certain psychological programming that we tell ourselves when we believe that there's no hope or love left, and then, the devil starts to manifest those natural thoughts as supernatural realities to our souls that concede us to spiritual bondage.

Spiritual bondage is the total state of being bound in sinful, evil ways and circumstances. This life is always chaotic and filled with problems. The bondage is a heartfelt, superficial, loveless life. Bondage creates loneliness and despair, and each of these is a true supernatural attack that starts to suffocate a person in a traumatic incident or abusive situation that keeps them from healing. As a result of total submission to bondage and hopelessness, we start to live behind a mask to conceal the feelings of loss and emptiness.

Spiritual bondage often grabs us when we are at our worst, which is why Jesus tells us to seek the kingdom of heaven first and everything will be added to us (Matthew 6:33; NKJV). Doing this helps us to withstand the spiritual attacks of the enemy. You see, sometimes we are led away by different motives that distract us from the will and plan that God has for us. We begin to believe that we have the power and strength within us to handle a difficult situation that presents itself in our lives when we are merely receptors of that situation; how we endure it often determines how fast we will overcome it. The Bible tells us in Proverbs 14:12 (NKJV) that "There is a way *that seems* right to a man, but its end *is* the way of death." Therefore, we have to be willing to bind our hearts to Christ so that we do not believe that we have all the answers or are capable of living in peace and harmony without Christ. We have to be willing to give up our "freewill" for God's will.

There is hope and mercy for all of us who have struggled and fallen. There is hope and peace in knowing that Christ has not left us or forsaken us in our circumstances. He boldly proclaimed to us that He cares for us. It took me some time to understand that it was His love and mercy *at my lowest* that kept me from harming or hurting myself. I had distant memories in my mind of a scripture that said, "*Let your* conduct *be* without covetousness; be content with such things as you have" (Hebrews 13:5; NKJV). The Bible already affirms, "I will never leave you nor forsake you" (Hebrews 13:5b; NKJV) and

"Be strong and courageous. Do not be afraid or terrified because of them, for the Lord your God goes with you; he will never leave you nor forsake you." (Deuteronomy 31:6; NIV)

Hope and love are so powerful. Hope allows us to see that there is light in dark places. Hope enlightens our purpose, purpose delivers an impact, and impact makes a difference. Love generates the strength and courage to stand up and be accountable for someone and something when it's been freely given and freely received. Ultimately, internalizing these actions brings us peace and joy when we finally understand that only what we do for Christ will last and the great price that God made to allow His only Son to stand as atonement for our sins.

The love of the Lord greatly reveals to us that no matter what we encounter in our lives, we are truly loved so much that if we give our lives to Christ, we will experience the joy and peace that exceed and heal all wounds that were self-inflicted, earned, or undeserved. He can remove our pain and emotional burdens and forgive them. Jesus is the Great Physician and loves each of us right where we are in our lives. Give it to Him; He cares and deeply wants to help. Please don't be afraid to seek Him when you are crying out for help. He wants to give you rest from your problems and pain. Christ became the pain, shame, and sickness that stretch across our past, present, and future when He hung on the cross at Calvary.

This is written in the Old Testament of Isaiah 53:3–6 (NKJV):

> "He is despised and rejected by men, A Man of sorrows and acquainted with grief. And we hid, as it were, our faces from Him; He was despised, and we did not esteem Him. Surely He has borne our griefs and carried our sorrows; yet we esteemed Him stricken, smitten by God, and afflicted. But He was wounded for our transgressions, He was bruised for our iniquities; the chastisement for our

peace was upon Him, and by His stripes we are healed.
All we like sheep have gone astray; we have turned, every
one, to his own way; and the LORD has laid on Him the
iniquity of us all."

So, you see, only Jesus Christ willingly accepted responsibility for
our sins and trials. He wanted to restore the supernatural and spiritual
balance that was missing in mankind from our birth to our deaths.
It is He who wants to bless us with abundant peace and joy. He did
not inflict any of those evil things to offset our lives. It wasn't him or
God who placed those curses or demonic and parasitic people in our
lives. Consequently, it was the inheritance of sin from Satan's plan
that causes us to experience death and destruction. Jesus wants to heal
us and restore the peace back into our lives which the devil has stolen
from us. He wants to love us and advocate for us to our Creator for
whatever shortcomings that we may encounter. It is the ultimate gift
of love and acceptance that helps us to receive His advocacy, because
while we may still be sinners, Christ still loves us.

I finally realized that His peace and love lifted me after I committed my life to Christ and accepted Him as my personal Savior to
rest, rule, and abide over me and my circumstances. Since that time,
I can say that I now have "that" Father's love I longed for. Now I have
that fatherly acceptance that I thirsted for so many years. My life and
heart were transformed and recreated through the infilling of the Holy
Spirit so that I could unconditionally love again. Jesus's example of love
and forgiveness rested in my heart and destroyed the barrier of pain
and hate that locked my heart in chains of bitterness and insecurity.
I know now what "with His stripes we are healed" means.

CHAPTER NINE

So Glad I Made It

"And He said to me, 'My grace is sufficient for you, for My strength is made perfect in weakness.' Therefore most gladly I will rather boast in my infirmities, that the power of Christ may rest upon me. Therefore I take pleasure in infirmities, in reproaches, in needs, in persecutions, in distresses, for Christ's sake. For when I am weak, then I am strong." (2 Corinthians 12:9–10; NKJV)

I made the decision to activate my faith and try something new by trusting God when He proclaimed to all that would listen, "Behold, I will do a new thing; now it shall spring forth; shall you not know it? I will even make a road in the wilderness and rivers in the desert" (Isaiah 43:19; NKJV).

My "desert" circumstance was my desire to be the best father and parent to my children. I desired to find a mate that would be the helper I needed to raise my children; however, this was a terrible mistake and a costly gamble because I slowly drifted further away from the blessings of obedience and found myself encapsulated in the curses of disobedience. My finances were cursed, my home was cursed, my job was cursed, and my family was stricken with illness and disease. I was in the wilderness and truly needed God's help and guidance, but I had to repent, deeply humble myself,

and ask the Lord God to create in me a clean heart and renew the
right spirit within me.

I had to understand what God had already told me if I wanted to
be His people: "If my people, who are called by my name, will humble
themselves, and pray, and seek my face, and turn from their wicked
ways; then I will hear from heaven, and will forgive their sin, and
will heal their land" (2 Chronicles 7:14; NKJV). It wasn't about me
and what I wanted or felt; it was all about God's requirements and
purpose for my life. Satan had me believing that I could live a life that
is displeasing to God and still be blessed. I was led to believe that I
could disobey the moral laws that God has given us that prepared us
to be living vessels of worship for His glory and still be fully blessed
with peace and joy, but that was a lie. I was also led to believe that
I could follow my own will and aspirations above God's plan and
purpose for my life and still be blessed, but the Bible clearly tells
me, "For I know the plans I have for you,' declares the Lord, 'plans
to prosper you and not to harm you, plans to give you hope and a
future" (Jeremiah 29:11; NIV) and "The blessing of the Lord makes
one rich, and He adds no sorrow with it" (Proverbs 10:22; NKJV). I
had to realize that there was so much more to God and His Son,
Jesus, than material things.

There is a majestic peace that surpasses all understanding and
it keeps your hearts and minds through Christ Jesus. What are you
waiting for? Jesus is waiting, and God has ordained it. Now all you
have to do is walk into it. "For God so loved the world that he gave
his only begotten Son, that whoever believes in him should not perish, but have everlasting life. For God did not send t his Son into the
world to condemn the world; but that the world through him might
be saved" (John 3:16–17; NKJV).

I am so glad I made it. When I say "it," for me, this is the decision
to live a life for Christ, to accept Him as my Savior to love others
enough to become a servant of Christ to serve others. I am also so

glad that I did not miss the calling on my life, for I was lost and hurting for years in the depravity of lust and sin until I couldn't hear my Shepherd's voice. That's not because He wasn't listening; it was because I wasn't calling Him. I truly understand the scripture in Proverbs 3:5–6 (NKJV) as it reads, "Trust in the Lord with all your heart; and lean not unto your own understanding. In all your ways acknowledge him, and he shall direct your paths."

Now I am so glad to make every effort to live every day to reverence God and avoid the appearance of evil in my life because I want to inherit the fullness of grace and love that God has for me. Jesus also loved me so much that He willingly gave His life for mine. So, I ask you, what more can Christ do to show you that He desires to love you, heal your pain, and take away your suffering? Go to Him with your broken heart, your downcast emotions, and your addictions and illness—He is waiting. Can you hear Him saying, "Come unto me, all you who labor and are heavy laden, and I will give you rest" (Matthew 11:28; NKJV)?

I am so glad I made it. I'm no longer bound to sinful shackles holding me down and pinning me in my guilt and shame. I'm free, and I've had that inner peace that rests, rules, and abides within my heart ever since I surrendered my existence to Jesus. God's grace is more than enough for all of us.

There are two scriptures that come to mind when I think of situations that can truly help put into perspective what we are experiencing. The first is found in Ephesians 6:12–13 (NKJV), where the Bible tells us that "we wrestle not against flesh and blood, but against principalities, against powers, against the rulers of the darkness of this world, against spiritual wickedness in high places. Wherefore take unto you the whole armor of God, that you may be able to withstand in the evil day, and having done all, to stand." Sometimes we are attacked early and often with different strategies from the devil to keep us trapped in supernatural bondage that robs us of the insight that illuminates solutions that we are more than conquerors in Christ, yet we fall prey to the principalities of spiritual wickedness in high places.

Everywhere we go, the enemy tries to place us in a spiritual stronghold that keeps us busy trying to figure out in our natural minds how to overcome the obstacles in our lives when Christ already told us that He is "the way, the truth, and the life" (John 14:6 NKJV). We cry and become depressed because we do not understand why the lives that God has given us are so hard. We become convinced our lives have to be filled with hurt and harmful situations because that's the way God may have intended for it to be. Someone stated on a television show, "Well, that's life! Get used to it!" This is not true. God created us in the image and likeness of Him. He has all power over heaven and earth. He did not create us to be gods or to desire to be gods; He strictly wants us to know that we can be reconciled back to the will of God. We are now able to speak to our situations with divine authority and zeal, knowing that the power of God is connected to our lives and that if we are living lives that are pleasing to Him, we can do all things by faith through Christ.

God loves us so much that He finds it so hard to turn away from us. He finds it hard to write us off as sinful again. You see, the Bible tells us that God destroyed mankind with a flood because of the enormous amount of sin and evil that enslaved the inhabitants of the earth. He essentially started over with mankind and allowed us to keep our freewill and willingness to choose through Noah and his family. That's why we are no longer captive or bound to sin because now we can individually choose to be saved.

God does not like us to live associated with the deceptive tricks of Satan. The sinful tricks of Satan want us to believe that we are eternally lost and there is no hope; and where there is no hope, people begin to lose their connection to God. The deceptions of sin are the broken obedience's of God set forth in the Old Testament scriptures of Exodus, Leviticus, and Deuteronomy. Many of the 613 Old Testament laws were created for man to help the chosen nation of Israel and others understand that there are higher standards and requirements of holiness and sanctification required by God. The laws were given because God wanted to reveal to anyone who believed that He is the one true God. Even today, the descendants of Ishmael still hold true to many of the Old Testament scriptures, and they govern their lands according to some of the Old Testament laws. God is a holy God, meaning He is sinless and just. Therefore, our lives and thoughts must become holy in order to be fully connected with Him.

In Leviticus 19:2 (NIV), God tells Moses, "Speak to the entire assembly of Israel and say to them: 'Be holy because I, the LORD your God, am holy." Some may argue that they, themselves are living a holy and sin-free life; and that Holiness living is easy with the Holy Spirit. That is true, however; can you honestly confirm that you've not broken ANY of these laws (Past or Present) in the following list: Do not embarrass others; Do not oppress the weak; Do not speak derogatorily of others; Do not take revenge; Do not bear a grudge; Do not follow the whims of your heart or what your eyes see; Do not inquire of spirits; Do not consult magicians or seers; Do not be superstitious; Do not engage in Astrology; Do not go into a trance to foresee events, etc.; Do not tattoo the skin; Men must not wear women's clothing; women must not wear men's clothing; Do not walk outside the city boundary on the Sabbath; Do not wear cloth woven of wool and linen. These are only 16 of the 613 laws and/or Commandments that are written in the Old Testament Scriptures that the Children of Israel was required to live by. That's why Paul asked the Galatians the question "Who have bewitched you?" Therefore, each of us needs this set of laws and consistencies to help govern our hearts into accepting the good news of the Gospel.

Our lives do not have to be filled with pain. Jesus told us that He came not to condemn the world but to set the captives free. In order for every person to be free from the grips of spiritual warfare, we must return to the place before the fall of man, before Adam disobeyed God, and before sin totally corrupted the world. We must return to our first love, which is the love of God. He created us so divinely, so uniquely, and so masterfully that the blueprint has never been recreated. We are the salt of the earth and the light of the world, and we must be willing to set aside every weight and sin that keeps us bound to our transgressions and stand in the newness of grace and mercy.

We were created by God to have dominion over everything on earth. Adam named every living thing on earth, and God placed Adam (man) over it all to look over it and to take care of it. God loves us and wants us to be abundantly blessed to fulfill the plan and purpose that we were created for. Since the creation of man, Satan has been filled with jealously and anger because God created earth for man and man to live and take lordship. Satan was angry and decided to deceive man and rob them of the plan and purpose that God had. This is very significant because we cannot fully walk into the blessings of God because of the living existence of sin that we allow to keep us disconnected.

Regardless of how much you have sinned in your life, no matter how many times you've broken God's laws and statues, I'm here to exclaim to you that as long as you are alive and still breathing, there is time to change your heart and repent to be redeemed. God loves us with an endless love, but He hates the sin that we have allowed ourselves and our hearts to be engulfed with. When you read the Bible, it tells us of so many times that God spared man from death because of their willingness to repent and ask for forgiveness from their hearts.

That's what it will take for everyone today. God clearly told us that if we repent and turn from our wicked ways, He will heal us. Jesus told us that if we believe on Him, repent, be baptized, and believe that He is the Redeemer, then we will be saved. That's why I am so glad to know that a merciful God loves me with an everlasting love and Christ died for my sinful self so that I may be redeemed into holiness through the events of His death, burial, and resurrection. It all starts with faith. I'm glad to know that it starts with faith and not works or indulgences to please God. The simplicity of accepting God's sovereignty and accepting Christ as our Savior is all about our faith.

All that Christ requires of us is to believe in our hearts that He is the Son of God and confess with our mouth that He is the Savior who died for our sins and rose from the grave to remain our intercessor and ultimate sacrifice for sin. Then, by faith, we understand that it is by His unmerited favor and love that we are now the redeemed. Ultimately, we must not take for granted the magnitude of this favor. He and God willingly sacrificed for each of us so that we can be reunited with the kingdom of God. Each of these actions are personal, individual acts of faith, and without faith, it is truly impossible to please God. Finally, always remember the scripture in Ephesians 2:8–9 (NKJV) as it clearly tells us that "For by grace you have been saved through faith, and that not of yourselves; *it is* the gift of God, not of works, lest anyone should boast." Will you exercise your faith today and accept the gift of salvation? Your gift is waiting for you to accept it.

CHAPTER TEN

Love Is the Reason

"But the end of all things is at hand; therefore be serious and watchful in your prayers. And above all things have fervent love for one another, for 'love will cover a multitude of sins.' *Be* hospitable to one another without grumbling. As each one has received a gift, minister it to one another, as good stewards of the manifold grace of God. If anyone speaks, *let him speak* as the oracles of God. If anyone ministers, *let him do it* as with the ability which God supplies, that in all things God may be glorified through Jesus Christ, to whom belong the glory and the dominion forever and ever. Amen." (1 Peter 4:7–11; NKJV)

Have you ever thought about the unique gifts that you have and the way that it draws people to your friendship? Have you noticed that people might come to you for advice or comfort when they are down or going through personal situations in their lives? Our gifts and talents have been given to us from God to be a blessing to Him. He created each of us with a spark or a gleam that reveals our true nature and divine purpose. We are separated this same way in Christ. When we use our talents to sing, it reveals the purpose that we were created to sing unto the Lord a new song that is pleasing to Him. Also, we should always give thanks and honor to God for giving us the gifts and talents that we share with the world.

Another way that our gifts can bring God glory is when we acknowledge Him for the opportunities to showcase our gifts to the world.

I know that some people often believe that it's not necessary to give thanks to our Creator for all things, but it is truly important to give thanks. We must honor God and love Him for the blessings that we are receiving and utilizing on this earth. I challenge you to search your heart and mind to find the passion and gift within you, and once you've found it, develop it and ask God to continue to allow your gift and talent to flourish. However, you must be willing to give it back to Him in homage or dedication. The Bible shows us how David played music so celestially unto the Lord until not only did it please God, but his music also had a profound calming effect on King Saul (1 Samuel 16).

God loves us so much He provided us with talents that make us special in life. He wanted us to know that all things given to us are "good" when it is offered to Him first. Now, don't misunderstand me. I'm not talking about the physical and monetary things that we acquire while we are alive; I'm talking about your heart and mind to bless Him as He continues to bless you. He wants to be first in our lives because He desires to protect and shield us from the hurtful things that sin has introduced into this world.

Love is the reason why we should worship and give our lives to the Lord. Some people may argue that "my gifts were cultivated" and "I worked hard to develop my gifts!" While that may be the case, God placed a remnant of your gift inside of you when you were created in His divinity so that one day you would find your gift and purpose and dedicate it back to Him in love.

Additionally, it also means that everyone has a uniqueness that God responds to when we worship and give thanks to Him from our hearts. Regardless, even if we live in the same social environment or are identical twins, there is something rare that separates and empowers us as individuals. For most of us, we were born into a family environment that surrounded us with love, joy, security, and happiness that helped us to grow and experience inner peace knowing that we didn't have to worry about our meals, where to lay our head to sleep, or if we were protected. In our childhood, we were able to touch things, feel things, and taste things that heightened our senses to the joy and beauties that the earth has to offer. Our nurturing family structure was there, protecting us when we were too naïve to see danger or harm.

Consequently, from this life learning extravaganza, we developed the understanding of how to like, love, and support others in return. Our natural love lessons determine how deeply we allow ourselves to live in peace and joy with Jesus. You see, this happens because the quality of love that each of us are exposed to throughout our lives provides us with a measuring scope of love for our own lives. I was around ten years old when I first started going to church. I can recall being a naïve young man who believed that everyone who went to church was "saved and filled with the Holy Ghost." That was the first time I witnessed more than two people acting joyfully happy to see each other.

My first experiences of unconditional love were my mother, grand-mother, aunt, and cousin, Norman, who loved me unconditionally and sacrificed so that I could have food to eat, a roof over my head, toys, and clothes to wear. This was a special parental type of love that looked beyond my faults to love me anyway. My sisters loved me unconditionally because we protected each other and shared good and bad times together. We helped each other prepare for school, shared food, laughed, and played with each other when no one else was around; we were there for each other. When times were hard and abusive situations reared their ugly heads in our lives, we held and comforted each other through the hurricane; we were able to watch the storm pass and the sun shine again. However, in each of our lives, there will be times when we start to forget how to hold on to the primitive bonds of love and support that we grew up clinging to. We will forget how to show unconditional love and trust those that smiled at us and will become passive to love and endearment to the point that we forget how to love and support those that were there for us early in life. This is the beginning of our degeneracy as men and women.

We were created to love and be loved. God created us in His image. Adam was given dominion over the entire earth, and he loved his position on earth; he named and loved every creature that was made by God. God and Adam walked together and talked about love, living, dominion, and peace. God vehemently expressed to Adam in love and authority, "Of every tree of the garden you may freely eat; but of the tree of the knowledge of good and evil you shall not eat, for in the day that you eat of it you shall surely die." (Genesis 2:17; NKJV).

Some may question the reasons why God planted that particular tree in the garden with two newly made people who only knew God. Maybe God was testing Adam to see if He would always be obedient to the voice of the Creator. Maybe man was destined to fail and fall because of the nature that we were created with. The nature that we were created with was the nature to help, nurture, support, worship, and love just as God. Genesis 1:26 (NKJV) tells us, "Then God said, Let us make man in our image, according to our likeness: and let them have dominion over the fish of the sea, over the birds of the air, and over the cattle, over all the earth, and over every creeping thing that creeps upon the earth."

God's image is the image of righteousness and truth. He is the joyful whisper in the still of the night that tells us that we are loved. God's image keeps us seeking His peace when our natural lives are filled with turmoil and insecurity. He wants us to make the choice to come back to Him in truthful worship. This worship can only be done when we are fully in sync emotionally and wholeheartedly and mentally ready to love Him. Many believe that "freewill" plays a definite role in our decisions. Even today, man has the freewill to choose life or death, love or hate, and peace or chaos. But if we were given a choice to love or remain committed, would we choose God?

We ultimately have the choice to love our Creator again and be restored to our rightful place of dominion over our lives through Him. Have you ever felt as if something or someone were leading you down a path to destruction? This feeling is the influences of sinful characteristics that tells us that it is all right to live and do things that keep us further from the purpose and divine plan of God. Just like Adam and Eve's fall in the past, we are equipped to fall as well because we are products of our past. Sin has been so instilled in our minds and hearts that it has become first or second nature to many of us because our social circles have created an environment that allows us to thrive in depravity. But we don't have to.

The Bible tells us that Jesus loves us so much He told us, "If you abide in Me, and My words abide in you, you will ask what you desire, and it shall be done for you"(John 15:7; NKJV). Once you take a personal look at the teachings of Christ, you will see that He loves us so much and wants us to find purpose, peace, and salvation. Each of us must develop and build a personal relationship with Christ through reading the Bible daily, praying to know God in Christ, and seeking to live a transformed, sin-free life. That means we will have our hearts and minds transformed to honor and praise God through the Holy Spirit so that we can teach others how to live a saved life and accept God's deliverance from the bondage of our past sin and shame.

Love is the reason why I serve Him today. I can remember when I needed deliverance from the sinful things that I was entangled in. I knew that with my sins, my heart and mind were not the heart and mind of Christ. I felt the supernatural tearing away of God's presence over my life as I fell from God's grace. Just like Adam, I was ashamed to the point of trying to hide my naked soul. My soul was naked because the supernatural covering of my Creator was no longer around me and my heart. The freewill of deceit, jealously, envy, anger, and lust began to attach themselves to my life. But God still loved me to the point that my sins were forgiven through Jesus and cast away from me as I began to seek His love with a praying spirit for God to "Create in me a clean heart, God; renew Your spirit in me. I am a sinner, and I'm so tired of dying every day. Lift me up from my sinful attitude. Have mercy on me, God! According to Your tender mercy, clean me from all the sins in my heart. I am humbling myself; I am turning from my wicked ways. I accept the gift of salvation from Your Son, Jesus, and I acknowledge Him as my Savior and Messiah because I need saving, I need mercy, and I need grace."

It was at that time I realized I was a complete and total mess! Due to my freewill, I had ruined my life. I wasn't happy anymore; I could not feel joy or belonging. I was spiritually and emotionally drained. I'm so thankful for the Word of God and the passage (Ezekiel 37:1–14; NKJV) it gives us when God spoke to one of His servants, Ezekiel, and asked the question in the midst of a valley of very dry bones, "Can these bones live?" Then, God told him to speak the Word of the Lord to these very dry bones with the renewing breath of the Word of God so that they may live.

I cried out to the Lord to speak to my heart, and He loved me enough to moisturize my bones with the renewing spirit of redemption, to quicken my bones, smearing them with grace and mercy, and, more importantly, to breathe the breath of life into my nostrils to flow through my soul and mind, simultaneously renewing and transforming them to understand that God loves me so much that He gave His Son as a paid ransom for my "free-willed" sins. I willfully committed my life at that point and became reborn under Christ.

Now I know, without a doubt, Jesus came so that I may have life and have it abundantly. Jesus told us that we can come to Him if we are hurting and in despair and He will give us rest. His love is the reason why I wake up with a renewed sense of belonging to something greater than myself. Before, I was selfish and disconnected with my "freewill," but if I needed Jesus to love me beyond my faults, then I must love others beyond their faults. The Bible tells us that there is no greater love than for a person to lay down his own life and worries to care for a friend in need. The greatest commandment is to love God with all your heart and to love your neighbor as yourself. Our love should extend far beyond the social circles and our families to stretch further beyond our concentric circles. The greatest gift that we can share with anyone is the fact that by grace through faith, we are saved through Christ.

Joshua showed each of us in the Old Testament scriptures how should we respond to our choices. He said, "And if it seems evil to you to serve the Lord, choose for yourselves this day whom you will serve, whether the gods which your fathers served that *were* on the other side of the River, or the gods of the Amorites, in whose land you dwell. But as for me and my house, we will serve the Lord." (Joshua 24:15; NKJV). Joshua willingly made the choice to stand up and proclaim that no matter what everyone was doing or what deity they were serving, he and everyone in his house were going to serve the Lord. He became the priest of his household and bloodline; he just covered them under the matchless power of God. Have we loved our family deeply enough to reach out to cover them under God's mercy? If not, now is the time.

Now I am certain that I want God's will to be done in my life. He loved me when I didn't love myself; He shielded my heart and mind when I threw them vicariously in all directions. I love God because He sent His Son to die for my life so that I may have life. This is the reason I love God: He loves me with an everlasting love that never dies. There's a way to leave sin and insecurity, and that way is to believe in Christ and understand that His love is greater than ours.

Think about it for a minute—we already have a spiritual blueprint that illustrates to us how to love, live, and have faith in something greater than our understanding. There's no material payment or super-natural deal that an individual could make in order to live according to God's purpose. God's plan and purpose have been designed to allow us to freely make the ancient choice that reverberates from ancient times to now. This choice is given to all walks of life and asks the age-old question, "What do you choose to believe?"

Mankind has always searched for a "Higher Power" and a divine purpose. Some of us have incorporated sorcery, witchcraft, pagan god worship, and even self-worship into our lives as believers, and some believers are looking for that encompassing love and acceptance from a divine source. Every nationality has a celestial belief in a higher power that was foretold through the centuries of his/her existence; however, has there been such a poignant writing comparable to the life of Jesus? I agree that there are historical writings about simi-lar people during that time who also performed miracles, cast out demons, and even healed sick people, but none are quite like Jesus's teachings, sacrificial death, burial, and resurrection. The willingness to be sacrificed reveals a love that is transcendent and everlasting, which is the reason why I believe that He is the Son of God and the last sacrifice for the sins of mankind. He made the ultimate sacrifice by decreeing to all of mankind, "No one can take my life from me. I sacrifice it voluntarily" (John 10:18; NIV) so that we "may have [life] more abundantly" (John 10:10)

Jesus is the way to forgiveness, and God loves us so much that He is not slow in keeping His promise that He will never leave us nor forsake us. He wants us to know that there's a certain amount of time set aside for each of us to come home and be His children again. He is patient with everyone as long as we live and move on this earth; it's His desire that no one should die in their sins or be lost in their "freewill." He has so much love for us and is giving us grace (unmerited favor) to come to repentance (2 Peter 3:9; NKJV).

CHAPTER ELEVEN

Leading Once You Are Called

"Then I heard the voice of the Lord saying, 'Whom shall I send? And who will go for us?' And I said, 'Here am I. Send me!'" (Isaiah 6:8; NIV)

"For God has not given us a spirit of fear, but of power and of love and of a sound mind." (2 Timothy 1:7; NKJV)

I can recall when I first enlisted in the US Army. I had to take an aptitude test called the "Armed Services Vocational Aptitude Battery" (ASVAB) in which we were asked a series of questions that measured our ability to follow instructions. This test was also instrumental in assigning your job placement and helping to place you in a job career where you had the best chance to contribute to the mission and plan for the military.

One important aspect of the enlistment process was the fact that we were not forced or coerced into enlistment and pledging our allegiance. Each of us were part of what is called an "All-Volunteer Army," meaning each person willingly committed themselves to a cause or movement greater than themselves. In the early years of Christianity, the Disciples of Christ were asked to do this when Jesus reached out and voluntarily commissioned them to "Follow Me." Each of the disciples willingly committed their heart and mind to the leadership and teachings of Jesus. They believed that the coming vision and mission were going to be greater than who they were before Christ. The great parallel to the military and Jesus is He wanted to teach and train each disciple to eventually be a leader. Every one of us has the ability to be a leader once we answer the call.

I can remember my military life as a private in the US Army; it was a trying time for me because it was scary and new with anticipation. I didn't know what to expect after joining. There were so many horror stories to indulge my thoughts into, and I was so young and naïve. There were times when I had second thoughts because of the negativity that I had encountered. My first duty station was in Germany during the Cold War era and the age of communism. None of my fellow soldiers really understood the magnitude of the job that we had just volunteered ourselves into, but we knew that it was larger than we were. I further understood this concept as I started to grow as a Christian; as I mentioned in an earlier chapter, surrendering our hearts and minds reveals our submission to Christ. There has to be growth as a Christian in order to learn. Now our submission has to grow into our commission and then our mission.

The early church encountered many obstacles and persecutions as it started to grow almost immediately after the death, resurrection, and ascension of Jesus. Peter and Paul were instrumental in continuing the teachings of Jesus by spreading the good news of salvation to the Jews and Gentiles. Many rulers who ruled at the time of the first church of Antioch believed in the concept that if they killed the leaders or oppress the believers of Jesus, then the movement would eventually cease. This started a cavalcade of killings of Christians for their beliefs. As a result, these believers became martyrs for their faith. They accepted the internal question in their hearts and minds that is similar to the question that is illustrated in Isaiah 6:8 (NIV): "Then I heard the voice of the Lord saying, 'Whom shall I send? And who will go for us?' And I said, 'Here am I. Send me!'" They understood there would be perilous times ahead and they may even be killed for their faith, but they didn't mind because they knew they were called for such a time as this. That time was to proclaim the mighty works of the Lord. This is similar to understanding that our lives in the military may be in danger as long as we put on the uniform and wear it honorably. Additionally, each person who accepts being a Christian must be willing to learn the details of our faith and not assume the answers. In the military, we were drilled and evaluated continuously in our duties and responsibilities. We often took part in training exercises to improve our knowledge, skills, and abilities of those duties to ensure that we were experts at defending our country during a time of war. Our skills were sharpened, and our understanding of the mission was clear and concise.

Just like our beliefs as Christians, Jesus provided us with very clear and concise instructions for believers: "And Jesus came and spoke to them, saying, 'All authority has been given to Me in heaven and on earth. Go therefore and make disciples of all the nations, baptizing them in the name of the Father and of the Son and of the Holy Spirit, teaching them to observe all things that I have commanded you; and lo, I am with you always, *even* to the end of the age.' Amen" (Matthew 28:18–20; NKJV). Jesus instructed us to go and tell others the good news of salvation and freedom from spiritual bondage and oppression while revealing to those that are hurting and seeking liberation that He is the way and loves them with an everlasting love.

We must be willing to commit our minds and hearts to sharpening our knowledge of Christ in order to be effective to the commission. This takes time and effort by building a personal relationship with Christ through His teachings and how He addressed certain situations. Christ wanted to let everyone know that He is the Lord of the Sabbath, the Great Physician, and the Great Reconciler of those who want to be saved and set free. I can recall the time when I answered my calling into ministry and became a servant for the Lord; this was the greatest time of my life because at one point in my life, I thought I had lived so badly in my sins that I had lost my opportunity to be forgiven by the Lord. However, I was so wrong because He revealed His loving message that He still loved me in my struggle and depravity. Jesus told me, through an apostle I had never met before, that "I didn't miss it." These were my deepest thoughts regarding my life and salvation. This message was sent to me through my wife, which she and I never discussed my thoughts about my believing that I missed my calling to ministry. You see, I grew up in church and knew that Jesus was the only way to salvation, yet I chose to walk away from that affirmation, to experience "life."

But then, after voluntarily living outside of divine fellowship with Jesus for sixteen years, I was being told that He still loves me and has work for me to do. The news sent chills throughout my body! I began to cry out, "Thank you, Lord!" My wife, Denise, kept asking me, "Why are you so happy and what does that mean?" I began to tell her my greatest fear was that I had thrown away God's love. I'm writing all this to let anyone who feels as if it's too late to return to Jesus that as long as you are alive, you haven't missed it. Now is the time to believe. Now is the time to know Christ. You know, the wonderful part about all this is that He will accept you just as you are. He will forgive you and love you through your pain and problems. Today, my commission from the Lord is to tell those that are wondering if God still loves them and if salvation in Christ still applies to broken saints and sinners that the answer is YES!

It took me six years to fully understand the commission of Christ because I lived so long under the conditioning of depravity until that was all that I knew. And within that time, there was a spiritual transformation within my heart and spirit and I received the Holy Spirit. What stifles some people when it comes to Christ is that they may not be willing to commit to studying the Bible for themselves. It is easier to go to a place of worship and listen to someone being used by the Holy Spirit teach who Christ is instead of being that person who the Holy Spirit now rests, rules, and abides within to lead and guide into all truth.

Many believers have become complacent in the fulfillment of the Great Commission to "Go" make disciples and baptize. This is a universal mandate for everyone who believes and acknowledges to others that they are a Christian. It's easier to do this when you have truly and completely experienced the love of Christ and the infilling of the Holy Spirit for yourself because we have the "Good News" to tell others through our life experiences and testimonials that there is hope.

When we begin to teach and tell others how to be set free from their situations, we plant the seeds of hope and salvation to those that need to feel the same love and acceptance that each of us felt when we accepted Christ and the Holy Spirit into our lives. We have to love everyone past their confinement so that we can plant or water the seed of salvation. This takes love, which is the second part of Christ's instructions to all who believe. A lawyer asked Jesus, "'Teacher, which *is* the great commandment in the law?' Jesus said to him, '"You shall love the Lord your God with all your heart, with all your soul, and with all your mind." This is *the* first and great commandment. And *the* second *is* like it: "You shall love your neighbor as yourself." On these two commandments hang all the Law and the Prophets'" (Matthew 22:36–40; NKJV). Jesus wanted to stress the fact that love must be the driving factor in our worship to God and must be our reason to reach out to anyone that is hurting.

When we are strong enough and ready to fulfill the Great Commission and the Great Commandment of Christ, we have to know that we have been sent to do the work of Christ through the Holy Spirit's guidance and leadership. This is confirmed in Jesus's announcement in Luke 4:18–19 (NKJV): "The Spirit of the Lord *is* upon Me, because He has anointed Me to preach the gospel to *the* poor; He has sent Me to heal the brokenhearted, to proclaim liberty to *the* captives and recovery of sight to *the* blind, *to* set at liberty those who are oppressed; to proclaim the acceptable year of the Lord."

Now is the time to believe that once we accept Christ as our Savior, we are being prepared as an important instrument of the Great Commission and Great Commandment for salvation and deliverance to the people in our lives. We cannot wait for man's authority and permission to follow Jesus; we must be ready to talk about the goodness of Jesus and all that He has done for us and through us. Think about it! God has already placed you in your own personal marketplace filled with people who need to hear the good news. In our jobs, at school, in public locations, anyplace that we frequent—these are our opportunities to show love and offer salvation. This is what the new Christians did after the time of Jesus's resurrection. This is still very powerful today. We can show Christ's teachings working in our lives, and we can reveal the comfort of the Holy Spirit in our daily walk as well. Overall, it's all about having a personal and spiritual commitment to reach the lost in love and without fear.

After I answered my calling to be a servant-minister for Christ, I can honestly say that not all days in the marketplace for souls have been smooth or well received. But I continued to press, pray, and persevere until my spiritual skin became thicker. I now understand that we are ministers of the Gospel and are all accountable to Christ. I am blessed that my wife, Denise, accepted her calling to be a beacon and servant for the Lord while moving forward in the spirit of Christ and gratefully answering the announcement, "send me."

We believe that our abilities to be effective in our gifts are primarily in evangelism, teaching, and outreach. It is our individual passion to be ministers that are approachable and willing to go to those that are hurting to offer prayer or give spiritual words of encouragement to them, regardless of their circumstances or physical predicaments. We believe that love, support, and nondoctrinal teachings of the Bible are very much needed for our society today. We pray that the

Holy Spirit will take control of our purpose while positioning us to be effective with our gifts and talents for the Lord. Soon we can begin to evangelize and pray for the people that the Lord places in our paths. We understand that our calling to serve the Lord is totally where we feel comfortable.

So many people have grown terribly despondent with the way Christianity has become since its institutionalization. The first church in Antioch was very connected to Jesus by fellowshipping, evangelism, and prayer as is recorded in Acts 2:40–47. This was their primary means of strength and encouragement within their community of believers.

Once you accept Christ as Lord of your life, you start to feel as if you belong and want to help others; this is because of the teachings that He stood for. Romans 6:23 (NKJV) tells us that God wanted us to embrace the fact that we can have life and not death through the blood and sacrifice of His Son. This gift is the sacrificial love of His Son as the perfect sacrifice for all of mankind's sins. Therefore, by accepting this gift, you are given eternal life through Christ Jesus.

Our lives should be examples of Christianity that complement God's Word. When God speaks to our hearts, He speaks in love and mercy. He wants us to know that we are not alone as we witness and offer salvation to the countless people we encounter throughout our renewed lives. I am reminded of the times when I would listen to the radio with my grandmother. Every week, we would listen to Reverend Ike and Reverend Al, radio evangelists. I remember listening to the many sermons which were great and full of fire and zeal. I would listen to how each of them had a unique way of expounding on the scriptures. Both of them were equally enjoyable and played "church" music in the background. I really felt like I was sitting right there worshipping with them in our home. Both of us truly enjoyed the programs all the way to the end. We would clap to the songs and say amen at the radio. Sometimes we would look at each other with peace, as if we were affirming that the presence of the Holy Spirit had just entered the room. It was uplifting and very different to know that God met us outside of the church; this was very significant to me as I grew to understand the scripture, "I will be with you always" (Matthew 28:20) I felt Him then and still feel Him now.

Sometimes at the end of the broadcast, we would hear them make an announcement regarding going on a mission to Europe or another country to bring the Gospel to others. They were on fire when they talked about how great it was to be a part of the Great Commission to go and share the gospel to people who didn't know Christ and to provide them with Bibles, food, clothing, and essential items while showing them love and kindness. This was truly a great and very personal way to help an unreached group of people. Still today, it is through these missions that people who once believed in other forms of worship can make the personal choice to accept God as the one true living God and Christ as their Savior. However, there are people today who are killing Christians and persecuting them for their beliefs. People are still dying for the sake of Christianity and Christ.

Today, we can see where justice and missions are truly needed in abundance. The mission for every believer must now start at home. Yes, home. I'm not talking about the streets of your communities; I'm talking about the individual homes where people are responsible for each other's action in society. Our mission as leaders who are called by Christ is to solidify the spirituality of the home by standing with the parents that love the Lord and are willing to teach their families how to love others and to be accountable to God first.

Now, I realize that the family structures has changed with the acceptance of single parenting, latchkey-kid syndrome, same-sex marriage, and the pandemic incarceration of young men to the prison systems; this is indicative of the end times that we live in. The Bible tells us that certain social events will occur that will tell everyone Jesus is returning to love and establish His new sinless, spirit-filled kingdom here on earth. In 2 Timothy 3:1–7 (NKJV), we read,

But know this, that in the last days perilous times will come: For men will be lovers of themselves, lovers of money, boasters, proud, blasphemers, disobedient to parents, unthankful, unholy, unloving, unforgiving, slanderers, without self-control, brutal, despisers of good, traitors, headstrong, haughty, lovers of pleasure rather than lovers of God, having a form of godliness but denying its power. And from such people turn away! For of this sort are those who creep into households and make captives of gullible women loaded down with sins, led away by various lusts, always learning and never able to come to the knowledge of the truth.

However, the moral foundational teachings of Christ and the Holy Bible should still be important in the home. We should hunger and thirst after the knowledge that will sustain our hearts and minds to love the Lord with all our hearts so that we don't sin against Him.

Timothy continues to encourage and impart affirmations of love and assurance in 2 Timothy 3:14–17 (NKJV):

But you must continue in the things which you have learned and been assured of, knowing from whom you have learned *them*, and that from childhood you have known the Holy Scriptures, which are able to make you wise for salvation through faith which is in Christ Jesus. All Scripture *is* given by inspiration of God, and *is* profitable for doctrine, for reproof, for correction, for instruction in righteousness, that the man of God may be complete, thoroughly equipped for every good work.

We must be willing to share Jesus, the Bible (scriptures), and God's purpose and plan for mankind with everyone. Once we are able to reconcile families back to God and fill that family unit with peace, love, and joy through the edification and instruction of the scriptures, then Christ can heal, deliver, and set them free from the entanglement of Satan's bondage. But it starts with us! We must be willing to meet the families where they are and not pass judgment on them or their situations in order to cultivate change.

Jesus walked and ate with all types and backgrounds of people who desired answers and healing for their hearts. He was more than happy to share His love and grace to all. He healed whomever He touched without question. But on one occasion, there was a woman with an issue of blood who pressed her way through a crowd and touched His clothes as an act of faith that she would be healed of her issue. Well, she was right! Her faith and persistence helped her to touch the hem of Christ's garment. She was at her point of no return, and at this time, her faith was activated. She pushed, struggled, and endured her situation in order to finally get to her healing. That's what we must start teaching in the marketplace; we must teach that Christ will always be just a press or a push away when you need Him. We must teach that Jesus can heal a family in turmoil or facing social and emotional problems. Leading as we are called means that we are willing to look at the families we know and share Jesus with them.

As leaders, we must not constrain ourselves to a building and believe that being a pastor is the ultimate position that Jesus wants us to have. Don't misunderstand me, Pastoring is very important and pastoral care is very much needed; however, everyone isn't called to be a pastor. That's why the Bible outlines the spiritual gifts as written in Ephesians 4:11–12 (NKJV): "And He Himself gave some *to be* apostles, some prophets, some evangelists, and some pastors and teachers, for the equipping of the saints for the work of ministry, for the edifying of the body of Christ."

Everyone has a spiritual gift, but in order to know what your gifts are when you become a true Christian, you must be spiritually and mentally reborn into the goodness and love of God's spiritual and original plan for your life. The spiritual gifts were given to us when we were born but won't be called into existence until we are free from the entanglement and bondages of sin and evil.

That is why it is important to understand that now is the time to believe. There is a great need for true believers who are willing to truly deny themselves of the lavishness of sin and turn from naturally sinful ways so that they can be the men and women God can talk to and use to help restore others. This is far deeper and even greater than a title or a position in a church or ministry. This is the acknowledgment and complete acceptance that you have given your total existence to loving and being an instrument of Christ. This is called discipleship. Discipleship is not works or keeping traditional protocol; it is a commitment to the mission and movement. Your power to walk into the gifts of the Spirit requires that you be filled with the Holy Spirit, and He will give you the necessary power to activate the gift that's lain dormant within you. Acts 1:8 (NKJV) tells us, "But you shall receive power when the Holy Spirit has come upon you; and you shall be witnesses to Me in Jerusalem, and in all Judea and Samaria, and to the end of the earth." Have you received since you believed?

Today, we have to be completely open to being transformed, reborn, renewed, and saved from our old habits or understandings about life. We have to realize that we are very limited without Christ in our lives. It may seem that we have a fulfilling life while working within our strengths and talents, but we can do greater things through Christ, who gives us an endless amount of power, love, and grace, provided we remember that He is our strength. When we accept our spiritual purpose in Christ, it may not look similar to anyone that you know. Your purpose may be to feed homeless families, play music, entertain others, or build things to help people. Your purpose could be to teach people, preach to others with a clarity or purpose, and evangelize with the power to prophesy, or restore those who come to your services.

Each of these gifts is greatly needed and none more important than another; the point of the mission of Christ is to have a mission and talent that's filled with love and grace toward others so that God's love for us is glorified in all that we do.

Once you really grasp the significance of glorifying God by loving people in their circumstances, He will reward you with more blessings because you are honoring Him with your service. In the Bible, the apostle Paul is very clear when he states the parameters of Christianity and living a life as a believer of the Gospel of Christ:

> "I may be able to speak the languages of men and even of angels, but if I do not have love, it will sound like noisy brass. If I have the gift of speaking God's Word and if I understand all secrets, but do not have love, I am nothing. If I know all things and if I have the gift of faith so I can move mountains, but do not have love, I am nothing. If I give everything I have to feed poor people and if I give my body to be burned, but do not have love, it will not help me. Love does not give up. Love is kind. Love is not jealous. Love does not put itself up as being important. Love has no pride. Love does not do the wrong thing. Love never thinks of itself. Love does not get angry. Love does not remember the suffering that comes from being hurt by someone. Love is not happy with sin. Love is happy with the truth. Love takes everything that comes without giving up. Love believes all things. Love hopes for all things. Love keeps on in all things. Love never comes to an end. The gift of speaking God's Word will come to an end. The gift of speaking in special sounds will be stopped. The gift of understanding will come to an end. For we only know a part now, and we speak only a part. When everything is perfect, then we will not need these

gifts that are not perfect. When I was a child, I spoke like a child. I thought like a child. I understood like a child. Now I am a man. I do not act like a child anymore. Now that which we see is as if we were looking in a broken mirror. But then we will see everything. Now I know only a part. But then I will know everything in a perfect way. That is how God knows me right now. And now we have these three: faith and hope and love, but the greatest of these is love." (1 Corinthians 13; NLV)

I believe that the very core and essence of Christianity is built on loving others, forgiveness, peace, grace, and helping others. This was the entire mission of Christ as He fulfilled God's loving plan for man. God loves us and desires to use us to tell others of His great love for them. He wants us to tell them, "You did not miss His love." As believers in Christ, we should always prepare ourselves to show love. This may get trying at times, and some people may not be receptive to your message or outreach at first, but just remember that you're not doing any of this for an audience—your audience consists of two: God and Jesus.

As I take this journey as a minister and leader in the body of Christ, I am mindful to always allow the Holy Spirit to place me in opportunities to plant seeds of faith that will take root into some person's life. I'm excited about the mission I've been given to teach, train, and help people who come to me for spiritual and everyday counseling. When I accepted my calling, it was a great day in my life. I can remember the moment I received the Lord's confirmation and commission. I was afraid and excited at the same time. This is what I prayed for as a young boy, but through the works of sin, I walked away and forgot how to return to Christ.

But I am so thankful that today I am able to see Jesus living in me through the power of the Holy Spirit. This keeps me uplifted and inspired because I believe I was really chosen to love those the Lord loves. It wasn't easy because I was presented with so many obstacles and snares that were almost impossible to overcome, but through it all, Christ was there. I remember the scripture that helped me to endure with hope and faith: "Yea, though I walk through the valley of the shadow of death, I will fear no evil; for You *are* with me; Your rod and Your staff, they comfort me" (Psalm 23:4; NKJV). During my walk with Christ, there have been times when I was stricken with illness that tested my faith and stretched thin, testing my understanding of the scriptures.

In August 2014, my wife and I were blessed to attend a prophetic conference in Atlanta, GA. During this period, we were told by the prophet that we were going to be attacked very hard by Satan within the next twenty-one days and that he was going to try to stop God's blessing for us. Sure enough, that's when the sickness began. Overseeing the prophetic conference was a prophet named Jasmine, a true prophet of God because *everything* that he prophesied to us surely came to pass!

In November 2014, Denise and I were instructed by the Holy Spirit to commit ourselves to a period of consecration unto the Lord. What this means is that we were giving up things or circumstances as an offering unto the Lord and a sacrifice for us. During the consecration times, you are to separate your heart and mind from the things of everyday life and devote special time and energy to hearing God speak to you. Also, your time should consist of reading the Bible and remaining spiritually connected to seeking God's purpose and plan that He has for you. You must also open your heart to the Holy Spirit's guidance and understanding your individual purpose. We sacrificed television and the internet during this time; we would only listen to praise, gospel, or melodic music to help us stay in a place of devotion. We truly appreciated the blessings of the Lord in our lives and marriage during this time. We felt an awakening of God's spirit and a refreshing of gifts moving within us that would help us to be effective leaders and ministers to the people He has assigned to our outreach and ministry. I felt very encouraged and strengthened. My heart was full of His love. However, the devil was listening and got busy really fast.

One evening, I was lying in bed asleep. It was around 3:30 a.m., and I had been sleep for some time. All of a sudden, I was awakened by the Lord because I thought I heard someone calling my name. "Thomas, Thomas, wake up." As I started to wake, I could feel my legs weakening and a feeling of agitation. Also, the right side of my face began to grow numb. I thought that this was my blood sugar level dropping, so I immediately went to check my sugar reading to see that it was 99. I went to the refrigerator to find a cup of juice to help raise my blood sugar level, but the Holy Spirit told me, "That's not all. Check your blood pressure!" I started to look for the portable blood pressure machine by my bed. At this time, Denise woke up to check on me and see if everything was fine.

"Babe, you okay?" she asked.

"No," I said. "I don't know what's happening; my face is numb and my sugar is low."

"What!" she exclaimed.

I got the blood pressure machine hooked up to my arm and began to check my vitals.

Denise began to notice that I was in distress and started calling out Jesus's name. "Jesus, Lord Jesus, help us!" The blood pressure machine stopped, and the reading was 187/137. "What is it, babe?" she asked, and I let her see the screen. "Jesus!" she screamed. "What should we do?"

"I'm not sure," I replied. The Holy Spirit told me to call 911, but before I could complete my sentence, Denise had already started dialing. I could feel my chest starting to feel like something was sitting on it. I started to cry out to the Lord in despair and anguish. As my wife started to tell the operator where to come, I started walking around in the living room, praying, and crying out to the Lord. "Please, dear God, not like this. I still have so much work that You've shown me that needs to be done. Please, God, let me live. Lord, I accept You as my Savior and I commit my life to You. Forgive me for all my sins and be my Savior."

Immediately, Denise started to pray! I looked over at her as she stood near me praying and exalting the name of Jesus. "Jesus, we bless Your name, Lord. We love You, and I need You to touch my husband's body, heal him, and keep him here until the paramedics arrive. I know that You can do all things. We ask that You come and see about us." She and I continued to pray with one voice and without ceasing because this was all that we knew to do at a time like this.

You see, just two months earlier, my wife had been stricken with hives so badly that the hives started to restrict her breathing. We prayed and petitioned Jesus from our souls to heal and deliver her from the hives, and we were able to get her to the hospital in time to be treated. We were in the emergency room three times in three days because her hives were so bad that there were pancake-size hives traveling throughout her body. I would rub her hives as she would pray that they would calm down or stop itching. My natural thoughts and feelings of hopelessness were telling me that there was nothing I could do; however, the Holy Spirit that rests and rules my heart told me otherwise! I began to speak the Word of God in Psalm 118:17 (NKJV) with authority over my life, "[You] shall not die, but live, and declare the works of the Lord." I kept saying that until the Holy Spirit told me to say that we may be hard pressed but not destroyed and never defeated. We kept praying and declaring victory over that situation until the Lord relieved her of the hives and they went away. Now, two months later, I was being rushed to the hospital with a blood pressure reading of 187/137 and a blood glucose reading of 99, all simultaneously.

This was a trying time for us; we felt weary and beat up, but our faith and trust in God remained strong. We began talking about the characters in the Bible who endured hardship and trials greater than ours and how they were still able to trust and have faith in God to see them through. We believed in the prophecy and the fact that we were told that this test would come. We would often seek prayers from our spiritual brother and sister, Bishop Carldale James and Evangelist Tahkesha James, founders of He's a Wonder Music Ministries of the Apostolic Faith, and the congregants. It was truly their faithful prayers and constant contact with us that galvanized our belief that ministry and "spiritual Christians" can—and should—pray, fellowship, and encourage each other, no matter where they are. We really needed a community of believers to be there for us and not look at us as if we were being "punished." We were not defeated or being punished; we were being refined and restructured during this time. God wanted us to endure this for a greater testimony of *Faith* and *Grace*.

Their congregation took us in and loved *on* us through our sickness and were real beacons of love and life to me and my wife during this time. They showed love and grace toward us after each attack and illness. We needed to feel protected, loved, and part of a band of people who didn't mind praying for and with us. We were strengthened by their faith because we missed that feeling. God bless you both, Bishop and Evangelist, as well as your congregation, for your pastoral care.

We were really tested pertaining the scripture, "for when I am weak, then I am strong" (2 Corinthians 12:10; NKJV). My wife and I simultaneously endured sickness, pain, isolation, and crime all while living in Georgia. This was during a time that we were very young in our ministry as pastors and leaders of Reflections of Grace Outreach Ministries. We were excited about the mission and vision. We would often wake up with anticipation and zeal, waiting for the opportunities God had in our paths to offer salvation to someone, anyone. We were just happy to answer the calling on our lives to reach the lost at any cost.

During our stay in Georgia, we noticed that there were some things that didn't quite seem right to us as we began to get settled. We noticed that some of the people who we randomly met were very cold and distant. We weren't sure if it was us or just the enemy trying to discourage us from walking in the ministry that we willingly accepted. We believed that the "South was very nice and hospitable"; however, all that we experienced from the majority of residents were very harsh and cold looks. We were blessed to meet remnants of the hospitable South, but we soon learned that the majority of the people there were not original Georgians. We were often blessed to have our cousin Amaris, the Actress, Producer, and Screenwriter, dropped by to spend time with us and give us encouragement. It truly was a welcomed relief during our test to see and hear a warm and inviting voice in the house. She brought rays of hope and fun whenever she would tell us about her acting opportunities or film debuts. We are so proud of her for constantly allowing God to order her steps, as well as pursuing her dream to become an actress. There's no doubt in my mind and heart that she will be great really soon. We love you, Amaris, and thank you for the compassion and love you showed us by checking in on the sick. You will always have a special place in our hearts. However, our stay in Georgia really tested our faith in people who relished in the fact that they were considered Christians; because, the remnants of Christ's teachings to "love our neighbors as ourselves" wasn't concise or pronounced to us at all. This started to really be a problem as we began to venture out to meet people and fellowship at some of the local churches in hopes of possibly meeting and introducing ourselves and the mission that God has given to us to serve under. Well, I will tell you that we were not received well at all. This was truly a disappointment because we thought that this was one of the hubs of the "Bible Belt" of evangelism. However, the only church that we attended and felt truly welcomed and blessed to fellowship with was First Baptist Church of Atlanta. They will always be considered a spiritual home for us.

This continued for most of the first year that we were trying to get to know people there, by attending church services at different locations, and we were never greeted or made to feel that "new visitors" were welcomed. All that we were able to see was the fact that all the doors and hearts of the people were deliberately turning from us. This was a test that kept us on our knees, asking God if this was where we should be and, if so, would there be anyone who would have a heart for us enough to at least fellowship and embrace the mission and vision that was poured into us to give to the people. As we prayed, God was continuously strengthening us as leaders. We understood that we had to rely and trust solely on the Word of God and Christ to lead and direct us through the Holy Spirit during this time. We prayed, "The Lord is our keeper." We proclaimed that the Lord was doing a new thing with us and that He would make a road in the wilderness and rivers in the desert. We started to cast all our cares on Christ and wait on the Holy Spirit to reveal God's plan more and more because we felt lonely and excluded from everyone there. It was a tough road of consecration and separation that we had to endure.

We constantly prayed and believed that God was pruning and sharpening us to do a great work, but we had to be reshaped and molded to be a man and woman of God who would be able to relate to those that were dealing with loneliness, isolation, and fear. The Lord was revealing to us that each emotion and thought we were feeling was representative of some people who we would be ministering to soon. We were experiencing church hurt for the first time, and now I can truly relate to the feelings of being cast aside and irrelevant. This was a great and painful learning experience. How could we be effective in our evangelism if we never experienced those feelings as well?

I'm reminded of a scripture that puts all this in perspective:

How then shall they call on Him in whom they have not believed? And how shall they believe in Him of whom they have not heard? And how shall they hear without a preacher? And how shall they preach unless they are sent? As it is written: "How beautiful are the feet of those who preach the gospel of peace, who bring glad tidings of good things!" (Romans 10:14–15; NKJV)

Our lives just seemed to be filled with chaos and strife. After every test was over, we had visited the emergency room fifteen times and accumulated over $16,000 in hospital debt. We were reminded of the Bible story of Job and the trials and tests that he endured. I felt that the Lord was with us, but we had to continually remind ourselves that God will never leave us or forsake us; and regardless of our circumstances, we trusted that the Lord was able to deliver us.

Even people who trust in God and believe that Christ rules over everything have moments of uncertainty during a trial or tribulation. It was a painful but very revealing experience to feel the crushing of my flesh knowing that we are weak. We tried everything inside us to be strong in our faith. However, God did for us just as He did for Abraham at a time of his extreme test of love and sacrifice; God sent Abraham a ram in the bush to be sacrificed instead of his son, Isaac. The Lord revealed something to us while we battled our illnesses: we must start to encourage, pray, worship, and praise Him through our circumstances.

Meanwhile, people started to ask us questions about our ministry, and we were happy to have clear and confident answers that always glorified God. However, this wasn't always the case; we would get looks of disapproval when we would start to explain that our mission was to help provide for the natural man so that the spirit man would be open to learning more about Christ.

We started to tell people that our ministry wasn't about an offering, a building, or a position. We were "seed planters" for the kingdom. We were evangelists in the marketplace for Jesus. We started to understand more clearly the purpose and plan He had for us as individual leaders for Christ and, at the same time, to solidify the promise that Reflections of Grace would be spiritually filled with the anointing and gifts that He predestined us to have in the body of Christ. The birthing of God's plan sometimes require labor pains and deep breathing during the delivery.

We noticed that whenever we started to do evangelism and outreach in Georgia, we were met with opposition. We started inviting people and groups to join us for corporate prayer and Bible enrichment via teleconference dial-in. We posted flyers, sent electronic invitations, and gave personal invites to join us for prayer and enrichment; still, nothing. After three months, we decided to seek the Lord for confirmation if we were supposed to be here witnessing and answering the call, "Here am I. Send me!"

We prayed and fasted through this time of testing and sharpening for confirmation and assurance from the Lord if this was His plan. And then, the Lord revealed to us that He would be with us and that we must still go into the marketplace to witness and help people know that God loves them and Jesus is the answer to their problems. We were essentially ministering to ourselves as Christ sharpened us through our evangelism. Reading the Bible and the stories of the men and women in the Bible helped us with understanding that our faith is what will keep us strong.

The Bible is so sweet and fulfilling when you are able to open it and feel the Holy Spirit in scripture. The Holy Spirit led me to a scripture in 2 Corinthians 4:8–12 (NKJV) as it ministered to my spirit to let me know

> *We are* hard-pressed on every side, yet not crushed; *we are* perplexed, but not in despair; persecuted, but not forsaken; struck down, but not destroyed—always carrying about in the body the dying of the Lord Jesus, that the life of Jesus also may be manifested in our body. For we who live are

always delivered to death for Jesus' sake, that the life of Jesus also may be manifested in our mortal flesh. So then death is working in us, but life in you.

This has become one my favorite scriptures because I believe that whatever situation I'm encountering, I just have to remember that Jesus is there. When I'm facing something that seems impossible, I have to know that all things are possible. I know that everything that I do for Christ must be covered by Him with His blessings and power. There has to be an un-relinquished solidarity that although times are hard right now, God will see me through it. When we are being led by God, there will be tough times that will cause you to pray harder and seek God's mercy. God wants us to want Him and seek Him when we are at our weakest points of service and honor toward Him.

Psalm 51:17 (NKJV) tells us, "The sacrifices of God *are* a broken spirit, a broken and a contrite heart—these, O God, you will not despise." Leading as we are called requires sacrifice and commitment to the cause of salvation. This cannot be a time for any man or woman to believe that it is their intellect or own self-willed determination that provides them with the strength and patience to love and reach out to those who are hurting and in dismay. It is the testimony and promise of God that He will never leave us or forsake us and that He will be with us always, even until the end of the earth. But we have to keep passing our tests and removing the earthly thoughts and feelings in order to connect with Christ on a spiritual and higher level through the Holy Spirit's comforting during our tests.

Leading as you are called after you've been through something keeps you grounded in knowing that if it weren't for God's tender mercies for us and His loving kindness to us, we might have given up. But we pressed when we were shaken, we prayed when we were perplexed, and we stretched forth our arms when we were hard-pressed to tell Jesus, "Where You lead me, I will follow. I give my life to You."

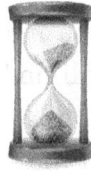

CHAPTER TWELVE

Standing the Pull While God Pulls You Through

"And He said to me, 'My grace is sufficient for you, for My strength is made perfect in weakness.' Therefore most gladly I will rather boast in my infirmities, that the power of Christ may rest upon me. Therefore I take pleasure in infirmities, in reproaches, in needs, in persecutions, in distresses, for Christ's sake. For when I am weak, then I am strong." (2 Corinthians 12:9–10; NKJV)

Religion is an important aspect in worship, and each believer has to make the decision to understand that God honors service and sacrifice for Him. Religion has the ability to organize people based on a collective, unified belief in an idea or worldview. Religion is a show of deep conviction and commitment to something. So, based on the definition of *religion*, a person can become a servant to the belief and not always the message. However, when you believe in the message of Christ, it gives you a chance to know how the Savior thinks, loves, and even cries. He has emotions and feelings that can be felt and understood by anyone who is willing to know who Jesus is personally and intimately. Jesus came to serve and encourage those that were looking for acceptance and peace. Jesus invited everyone to "Come to Me, all *you* who labor and are heavy laden, and I will give you rest. Take My yoke upon you and learn from Me, for I am gentle and lowly in heart, and you will find rest for your souls" (Matthew 11:28–29; NKJV). The yoke of Christ simply means that it is the message of love and freedom from the law (Galatians 5:1); the message leads and guides us to understand God's plan, as well as teaches us how to freely walk in obedience toward salvation.

Jesus was a great example of standing the pull when times were difficult in His life. When He was faced with death on a cross prepared by His enemies, He cried out loudly, "My God, My God, why have You forsaken me?" (Matthew 27:45–46; NKJV). His feelings and emotions were as real as yours and mine. Christ also prayed so hard to God until His sweat started to fall as drops of blood. Remember Paul? Paul was beaten many times and thrown into prison until he ultimately died as a prisoner for his faith in Christ. Now, I understand that these two examples are totally the exceptions and not the rule; however, there are many other ancient heroes, such as Perpetua and Felicity, Origen, and Euphemia of the second to fourth centuries. The persecution continued from the fifth century until the fifteenth century with King Edward the Martyr, Tsar Lazar, and Saint Joan of Arc. Lastly, in the modern era, Christians are still being persecuted for their faith. Currently, in the Middle East and Asia, Christians are systematically being killed and persecuted because they are not ashamed of Christ.

Jesus pardoned a thief's sin and affirmed to the thief that "today you shall be with Me in Paradise" because the thief was able to understand that the Messiah's death was greater than any situation or circumstance he was currently facing. (Luke 23:39–43; NKJV) We must believe deeply that there is nothing too hard for God and that our faith will initiate supernatural power which will open up the windows of heaven toward us and our circumstances to keep and shield us from destruction.

We must be willing to go all the way with Jesus in faith. Once we are transformed through the infilling of the Holy Spirit, we can better see the rainbow on the horizon instead of the clouds and storms we are in. The Bible proclaims we can find supernatural faith and trust if we lift up our eyes through our situation, knowing that our help comes from the Lord, who made heaven and earth.

When troubles and persecutions come into our lives, we must be willing to stand on the promise of our faith that God will be with us and the Holy Spirit will protect and instruct us through the pain and trials that we are enduring. I have to tell you that it won't be easy to stand in a spiritual warfare hurricane and it's not going to be easy to remember a scripture that will bring you comfort and peace during that time. When you see your life collapsing all around you, you may not feel the presence of the Lord all the time shielding you from your own thoughts and feelings, but you have to still look to Jesus, trust Him, and believe that He is still covering you from a much harsher situation than what you're experiencing at that moment.

In Acts 7, we learn of Deacon Stephen, who is considered to be the first Christian martyr. Stephen preached to the Sanhedrin counsel the fact that Jesus did not come to destroy the laws of Moses but to fulfill them. He called them "stiff-necked," which was the same description that God used concerning the children of Israel because of their desire to serve pagan gods (2 Chronicles 30). Stephen basically "called out" the Jewish leaders for their wrong doing and the fact that God does not only dwell in a particular building or structures. God is a spirit that dwells with those who are truthful with their worship. However, the leaders were so angry with Him that they accused him of blasphemy and stoned him to death. But if I could leave you with a relevant thought regarding the life of Stephen, it's this: he was still able to pray to the Lord, "'Lord, do not charge them with this sin.' And when he had said this, he fell asleep" (Acts 7:60; NIV).

You see, in Stephen's most difficult moment and eventual death, he was still able to find enough strength to show love, peace, and compassion to forgive those that hated him. What do we do when adversities start to overtake our lives? How do we cope with the loss of a loved one if they are killed at the hands of careless people? What would be our reaction if we were being destroyed by lies, deceit, and hatred? Are we willing to find strength in our faith to believe that something greater is waiting for us if we hold on and understand that when we are naturally weak in our hearts, then spiritually, through our faith, we are stronger to believe that no weapon formed against us will overtake our lives because we are more than conquerors in Christ? Stephen understood the facts of the good news that Jesus died and rose from the grave. He believed that Jesus Christ is the fulfillment of the moral laws and prophecies of the Messiah's coming. He also understood that Christ was seated back at the right hand of the Father, the God of Abraham, Isaac, and Jacob, as the advocate, intercessor and the author and finisher of our faith.

Someone reading this might start to think that everything written up to this point was easier to understand, but now we are supposed to give our lives to Christ to cover our hearts and minds in Jesus's name; this "covering in Jesus name" is a little too hard to believe or understand. The Bible tells us, "cast all your anxiety on him for he cares for you" (1 Peter 5:7; NIV). This is powerful because He wants us to grab the concept of faith and trust because that's what can transform a person's heart and tear down the feelings of doubt, mistrust, and unbelief.

You see, we need a spiritual, eye-opening experience with Christ in order to understand who Christ is. This cannot be understood with a mindset of logic or reasoning. That is why the Bible tells us to not allow our hearts to be troubled or to be occupied with problems or circumstances. Jesus wants to strip each burden and pain from our existence and leave our hearts unprotected and vulnerable just long enough to believe that He is the Son of God and loves us enough to protect our hearts with the Holy Spirit. This would be so hard to understand if you have not fully accepted the gift of salvation. We must be willing to release all doubts and fears and completely trust that Jesus is the divine way and at His name everything is subject to His authority. The Bible tells us in Colossians 1:13–17 (NKJV),

> He has delivered us from the power of darkness and conveyed *us* into the kingdom of the Son of His love, in whom we have redemption through His blood, the forgiveness of sins. He is the image of the invisible God, the firstborn over all creation. For by Him all things were created that are in heaven and that are on earth, visible and invisible, whether thrones or dominions or principalities or powers. All things were created through Him and for Him. And He is before all things, and in Him all things consist.

This is telling us that Jesus loves us so much and is able to fix our hearts, mend our lives, and restore the joy back into our lives; all we have to do is receive the Holy Spirit.

GRACE

CHAPTER THIRTEEN

It's Not a Religion but a Relationship

"For by grace you have been saved through faith, and that not of yourselves; *it is* the gift of God, not of works, lest anyone should boast." (Ephesians 2:8–9; NKJV)

During the early stages of our religion, Christians were considered radicals and militants against a Roman Empire who practiced pagan worship. Roman governors saw a change in the attitudes of the citizens of their cities and were afraid; the rulers decided to quiet them to the point of killing anyone who revealed that they were believers in Jesus.

Additionally, before Christianity and the church were established, Jerusalem had a large population of Jewish people living there and their primary religion was Judaism. They built temples and synagogues where they worshipped the God of Abraham, Isaac, and Jacob by upholding the scriptures, rules, and commandments of the Jewish scriptures called the Septuagint or Old Greek. Within some of these writings were the laws and commandments that eventually became the Old Testament. The Jews were primarily self-contained and compliant to the rules and laws of the government, as long as they were allowed to worship God without restrictions.

The Jewish people were essentially a nation within an empire and assisted the Roman government with keeping the peace within the Jewish communities through the written laws and scriptural text of the Old Greek. There were other religions and nations of people in Jerusalem that worshipped and believed in other versions of "true religion," yet people began to feel the empowering anticipation of the one true God's presence among them when Jesus began teaching and ministering to them. As a result, in the early stages of Christ's ministry, there was only a remnant of the Jewish people who embraced His teachings and affirmed that He was the Son of God. They were the beacons of hope and deliverance in the city. The people knew that something had to change after four hundred years of oppression, persecution, and seeking the Messiah for their freedom. Christ was teaching freedom and blessings, and all they had to do was believe that He was sent by God to "*To* set at liberty those who are oppressed (The Jewish people)" (Luke 4:18 NKJV)

When Jesus started His ministry, there was a celestial event happening that sparked the beginning of a new and exciting time in the Jewish culture. Some of the Jewish people quickly began to believe that Jesus was the Messiah and that He was the deliverer of God's chosen people from the rule of the Romans. Among them were twelve men who were known as Jesus's disciples, and they were committed followers of Christ's teachings. Signs, wonders, and miracles followed Jesus, and His teachings were instrumental in transforming thousands of people's hearts to have hope in a new day of peace, love, and joy.

What I love about the twelve disciples is the fact that each of them was an ordinary man chosen by Jesus to be a part of a paradigm shift that would evolve into a world religion. Each of them is a portrayal of us as we accept our lives as Christians. Sometimes we may be faced with the question of being adequate enough to be effective teachers or witnesses for Christ.

Each of them was special in his own way. They were unique and willing to follow Jesus no matter the cost. The wonderful thing about knowing this is that we can be assured Christ will use us to do a great work for the kingdom. Even if we are not well prepared or adequately taught the ins and outs, Jesus just requires that we be willing followers and that we be willing to share the Gospel with anyone and everyone. We must be willing to give it all up so that Christ can restore, deliver, and emancipate our minds and hearts to the leadership of the Holy Spirit. Almost every ruler during that time wanted to control the hearts and minds of this new movement, or "sect," that was rapidly growing momentum throughout the empire. Ultimately, when the leaders could not contain Jesus, they crucified Him on a cross.

After Jesus was crucified, the leaders believed this would end the anticipated hope of freedom that was spreading rapidly by the knowledge of Jesus's death. Many of the people who actually heard Jesus's sermons and parables realized, "This man is special." And as a result, they continued to teach and spread the message of Christ that He is the Passover Lamb slain. Christ was resurrected from the grave, and for forty days, He continued to provide final teachings to His disciples until His ascension to heaven (Acts 1:1–18).

Jesus's teachings and miracles touched many lives. Even today, the teachings of Jesus are still very life changing and powerfully relevant among millions who internalize the message. Jesus preached and taught about having faith and believing that a kingdom of God would be established on earth if they kept the faith and took to heart everything that He taught. He did not hesitate to promise them a life filled with greater. He promised that while they waited and endured the coming struggles, He would send a comforter and an instructor to lead and guide them through the difficult days ahead. All they had to do was "believe and receive."

The teachings of Jesus transcended the scriptures of the Old Testament because they allowed people to feel the message of faith instead of just hearing the message of faith. You see, Christ knew that there would be a time when people would not be able to physically see Him and would need to have faith and believe in the promise that He told would surely come to them. That promise will connect their hearts and spirits to understanding God's plan. He promised to send the Holy Spirit to help them manage their lives and purpose when they felt like giving up; He promised a keeper to keep them from living a life that opposes the teachings and standards of God.

Religion may require you to acknowledge that you belong and are committed to the teaching and the tradition of service and works on behalf of your faith in Jesus. Religion can cause a person to be easily persuaded to think that they are greater or more deserving of God's worship because they are in a position of authority, yet they forget that religion has no power without the supernatural connection to the Spirit of God, who brings about a change from the heart. Jesus promised to help mankind rekindle a personal relationship with God through Him. He tells us in John 14:6 (NKJV), "I am the way, the truth, and the life. No one comes to the Father except through me." It's simple: Jesus was telling everyone that their works or their religious acts or traditions weren't good enough to see the Father.

Sometimes we misunderstand the reasons why we go to church and fellowship as believers; there are so many traditional adaptations that we've incorporated in our service that borders on "ritualistic practices." Some churches require that certain clothes or colors be worn to church, they require that certain protocols must be followed in order for the Spirit of God to dwell in the service, and, lastly, they make monetary offerings and tithes a major focal point of service and not the call to salvation, sermons, prayer, and testimonies. I remember going to church as a young man and enjoying "Testimony Service"—this was a time when people in the congregation would be allowed time to share with others the blessings and miracles of God in their lives. This was truly encouraging because we were able to be witnesses of the power of prayer and the Spirit of God still moving and blessing His children on the earth.

Revelation 12:10–11 (NKJV) gives us a clear understanding that a testimony is important to overcoming current and past situations, as it is recorded by the writer, the Apostle John:

> "Then I heard a loud voice saying in heaven, 'Now salvation, and strength, and the kingdom of our God, and the power of His Christ have come, for the accuser of our brethren, who accused them before our God day and night, has been cast down. And they overcame him by the blood of the Lamb and by the word of their testimony, and they did not love their lives to the death."

If we were to look at the Bible from Genesis to Revelation, we would be able to summarize it into one word, and that word is *relationship*. God had a perfect functioning relationship with each of the people, prophets, and leaders in both testaments. It is important to recognize that it takes a relationship that's foundationally strong and without discourse to make something spectacular and long lasting happen. If we take the time to understand that God is a *community* of being within the mystery of the divine Trinity, meaning the Godhead for which we know as God the Father, God the Son, and God the Holy Spirit; The Trinity, existed in perfect mutual love. Through accepting this lasting relationship that is foundational in perfect mutual love, we can begin to apply this concept to our everyday "horizontal relationship" on this earth so they can grow and remain filled with love. As I mentioned, horizontal relationships are simply natural relationships that are mainly human in nature, are with other people, and are mostly for enjoyment, fellowship, and intimacy. However, God also desires that we apply these same aspirations to building a vertical relationship with Him. This can be done with fewer physical abilities and more spiritual attributes that we can hold fast to in our daily lives. A relationship with God needs to be cultivated and groomed through building and establishing a good prayer and worship life. Each individual must seek to worship God with their heart and mind by transforming their horizontal relational priorities more toward a better vertical overarching appreciation and devotion to pleasing God.

The relationship that each Christian should strive for is the relationship to hear and read the message of Jesus in the scripture and apply it to our lives in order to live and walk as new creatures that are freed from the bondage of our natural birth and be water baptized, submerged as a public announcement that we are believers in Jesus. Secondly, we are prepared to give our hearts and old souls to God in exchange for the restorative power of the Holy Spirit of God, back into our hearts. Also, it is the beginning process of searching and internalizing that we are emotionally and spiritually connected to the magnitude of the sacrifice that Jesus made for us. It has to be every individual's willingness to accept Christ as the atonement and intercessor for their sins and to strive to build a personal relationship with Him by acknowledging Him in our prayers and turning away from doing things that defile our relationship with God. We must be willing to search our hearts and minds to see if there's anything that we are doing that may be displeasing to God or if there's something or some thoughts that we need forgiveness for.

This is how you begin to build a concrete relationship in Christ by first decreasing the indulgences of sin. The Bible clearly outlines what God considers sin: "Now the works of the flesh are evident: sexual immorality, impurity, sensuality, idolatry, sorcery, enmity, strife, jealousy, fits of anger, rivalries, dissensions, divisions, envy, drunkenness, orgies, and things like these. I warn you, as I warned you before, that those who do such things will not inherit the kingdom of

God" (Galatians 5:19–21; ESV). When we are ready for a relationship with Christ, we are ready to give up the "works of the flesh" for that new and fresh restoration of peace and joy found in Jesus Christ. This peace and joy happens when we surrender our hearts to the Holy Spirit. Therefore, after this, we are infilled with the Holy Spirit of God to live a life that reveals Christ in our daily walk so that others will want to know "what keeps us happy and at peace."

We are no longer bound by our fleshly thoughts and dreams because our eternity has been sealed through our relationship and acceptance of the death, burial, and resurrection of Jesus Christ. We must be willing to tell the truth about salvation. The definition of salvation comes from the Latin word *savatio*, the Greek translation *soteria*, and the Hebrew word *yeshu'ah*, meaning to be saved or protected from harm or being saved or delivered from a dire situation. When we think of salvation in either of these terms, we see that there is hope and deliverance waiting for everyone who accepts God's gift of salvation. Therefore, we must believe with all our hearts that Jesus was not a liar or a Man driven by ambitions to be a religious leader with authority and pride. Jesus told everyone that He is "the way" and that the unfailing love, forgiveness, and joy are always available to help us, but all this must come first by being born again through allowing the Holy Spirit into our hearts.

Salvation comes by having faith in the message that Christ is the way. Faith comes by understanding the teachings of Christ and understanding what the Old Testament scripture proclaims in Joel 2:28 (NKJV), "And it shall come to pass afterward that I will pour out My Spirit on all flesh; your sons and your daughters shall prophesy, your old men shall dream dreams, your young men shall see visions." Jesus affirms this with the Great Commission in Matthew 28:18–19 (NKJV), "All authority has been given to Me in heaven and on earth. Go therefore and make disciples of all the nations, baptizing them in the name of the Father and of the Son and of the Holy Spirit."

In order to build a solid relationship with Christ, we must remain vigilant to biblical teachings that faith, salvation, and grace are all personal commitments that keep our relationship with Christ growing and filled with love through the Holy Spirit. The Holy Spirit gives us the insight to pursue clarity and the understanding of God's will and purpose for our lives. It's not about the gifts of the Spirit (right now) because new believers are still being taught what it means to live saved and free from sin. Leaders can sometimes "push by force" the Holy Spirit on their congregants. They tell them that they need the Holy Spirit, but they fail to take them through the process of repentance, explaining our faith, and offering salvation through Jesus.

Religion has been the dividing factor within the Christian community due to the different religious views on salvation, faith, and doctrine. After the apostles established the original churches, there were no dominations or even established church buildings. The believers came together in homes or other specified locations. Christians welcomed all who believed in Jesus and were willing to help expand the teachings of Christ to others. However, during the third century and after, institutionalization started to establish the church by incorporating doctrine and order. The churches of that time built religious orders and precedence's for everyone to follow, but they lost focus on the main reason why Christianity began. They forgot about Christ.

Unfortunately, not much has changed today. We have witnessed the great division of our faith that has greatly separated Christians to the point that we have discouraged people who once were seeking Christ to turn to other beliefs because the message of Christ has been absent in our evangelism.

Back in the early beginnings of Christianity, the apostles Peter and Paul were considered major proponents of our faith. Peter established our faith in Jerusalem and the surrounding cities. He taught Jesus and salvation to many of the Jewish societies and Judaic believers with the commission to proclaim to them that the "Christ" whom they crucified was, in fact, the Messiah that they were waiting for as proclaimed in Isaiah 11 and Jeremiah 23. The apostle Peter's teachings included the statement that each of them had to be baptized as is recorded in Acts 2:38 (NKJV): "Then Peter said to them, 'Repent, and let every one of you be baptized in the name of Jesus Christ for the remission of sins; and you shall receive the gift of the Holy Spirit.'" This is powerful because the Jewish and Judaic believers did not want to believe that Jesus Christ was the Messiah. They didn't want to believe that the Savior they had been waiting so long for they had just crucified; however, Peter knew that their acceptance of being baptized in Jesus's name for the remission of their sins would proclaim that Jesus is the long-awaited Messiah.

Peter also states to them in Acts 4:10–14 (NKJV),

Let it be known to you all, and to all the people of Israel, that by the name of Jesus Christ of Nazareth, whom you crucified, whom God raised from the dead, by Him this man stands here before you whole. This is the "stone which was rejected by you builders, which has become the chief cornerstone." Nor is there salvation in any other, for there is no other name under heaven given among men by which we must be saved. Now when they saw the boldness of Peter and John, and perceived that they were uneducated and untrained men, they marveled. And they realized that they had been with Jesus. And seeing the man who had been healed standing with them, they could say nothing against it.

Jesus, at the time of His ascension to heaven, states to the disciples in Matthew 28:18–20 (NKJV), "All authority has been given to me in heaven and on earth. Go therefore and make disciples of all the nations, baptizing them in the name of the Father and of the Son and of the Holy Spirit, teaching them to observe all things that I have commanded you; and lo, I am with you always, *even* to the end of the age.' Amen."

Consequently, Peter was bringing home the point that while they worshiped God and looked for the foundational truths of their faith in the buildings and structures, Jesus Christ was the main foundation that they were looking for as He preached and taught in the streets of the cities. Christ's teachings were a culmination of Old Testament scriptures that the Jewish leaders studied daily. Jesus Christ's teachings and spirit were the cornerstone to salvation and freedom from oppression and chaos in the lives of every person living; all they needed to do was accept it and begin to build their temple teachings on the teachings of Jesus and believe and proclaim that Jesus is the Messiah. But the Jewish leaders' hearts were hardened and they did not want a relationship with Jesus because the arrival of Jesus wasn't what they believed it should have been. Many times, people today misjudge Jesus because His introduction to them in their lives doesn't live up to the preconceived image of a "Messiah," and for this reason, they reject Him.

The Apostle Paul traveled and evangelized many countries that were not of Jewish descent; he zealously went forth, proclaiming and establishing the teachings of Christ. Paul taught that there is liberty in Christ and that salvation comes by grace through faith. His teachings were meant to help all people understand that regardless of their lives or lifestyles, they can have salvation, freedom, and deliverance through repentance, but first, they must connect with Christ through a spiritual rebirth that helps to build a personal relationship with Jesus Christ.

Paul also baptized in Jesus's name, as outlined in Acts 19:1–6 (NKJV), which tells us when Paul was in Ephesus, he found disciples there and said to them,

"Did you receive the Holy Spirit when you believed?"
So they said to him, "We have not so much as heard

whether there is a Holy Spirit." And he said to them, "Into what then were you baptized?" So they said, "Into John's baptism." Then Paul said, "John indeed baptized with a baptism of repentance, saying to the people that they should believe on Him who would come after him, that is, on Christ Jesus." When they heard *this*, they were baptized in the name of the Lord Jesus. And when Paul had laid hands on them, the Holy Spirit came upon them, and they spoke with tongues and prophesied.

I am making this point with the Apostles Peter and Paul because today, there's a doctrinal division with regards to the correct manner of baptism and in which is right and acceptable for salvation. As outlined in the biblical text, both are consistent to the fact that Jesus saves. If we look further into the message of that Jesus commissioned each believer at the time of his ascension in Matthew 28:18–20; again, Jesus was commissioning everyone who believed that He is Lord to Go and make disciples and "Baptize them in the name of the Father, the Son, and the Holy Spirit." This should be the foundational importance of our worship, praise, and devotion to our faith. Without Jesus, we are not Christians; also, without believing and building a personal relationship with Christ through our worship, we are still worshiping many gods and living a life that needs repentance.

That is why it is important not to rule out being baptized with the "baptism of repentance" (the Father, the Son, and the Holy Ghost) because John the Baptist, was chosen by God to be the forerunner and messenger for Christ. His only purpose and message while on earth was to tell everyone that the time of the Messiah and Savior was upon them. He preached repentance by vocalizing the need for a physical outward acknowledgment of their sins that held them captive for 400 plus years which scholars call it the "Years of Silence." The Jewish people and many of the other nations were very sinful and prideful.

John's message of repentance was God's way of preparing them and all of mankind back into fellowship with Him. Isaiah 40:3 says "The voice of one crying in the wilderness: "Prepare the way of the Lord; Make straight in the desert a highway for our God." Preparing the way for the Lord meant that everyone had to turn from their evil ways and heed to the message of John the Baptist, which was to repent.

Repentance allows a person to cry out to God to tell Him that you are personally sorry for disobeying His plan and will for your life. Repentance means that you are willing to change your heart and mind from disobedience and start a new direction of obedience and healing with God's spiritual guidance. 2 Chronicles 7:14 NKJV gives us God's definition of repentance when He tells us plainly "if My people who are called by My name will *humble themselves*, and *pray* and *seek My face*, and *turn from their wicked ways*, then I will hear from heaven, and will forgive their sin and heal their land. Depending on where you are spiritually as a believer, you should know deep down within your heart that you have repented and you are ready to commit your life to God in the spirit of holiness. Although, different denominations may preach or teach that a *specific* ordinance of baptism is right; meaning, some churches believe that you must be water baptized in Jesus Name in order to be saved; another believes that you must be water baptized in Jesus Name and filled with the gift of tongues soon after coming up from the water to validate your salvation, and lastly, another denomination believes that being baptized in the name of the Father, the Son, and the Holy Spirit is more than enough. But, let's ask ourselves the question; "What did Jesus Say? *"Go therefore and make disciples of all the nations, baptizing them in the name of the Father and of the Son and of the Holy Spirit*, teaching them to observe all things that I have commanded you; and lo, I am with you always, *even* to the end of the age.' Amen." Doesn't this statement answer all questions relating to baptism? Baptism should be given only once when the individual believes that he or she has truly and sincerely repented of all of their sins. Ultimately, it is the mind and heart of that individual who has personally accepted Christ as their Savior that repents. The infilling of the Holy Spirit is what keeps a person in divine fellowship with God's plan and purpose for their lives after baptism. And this can only be done by building a spiritual foundation through prayer, fasting, bible study, worship and being involved in a fellowship that builds your understanding of God and Christ. Also, it is the cleansing of the Holy Spirit that baptizes the believer with the anointing of the gifts of the Spirit as outlined in 1 Corinthians 12:1–31 and Ephesians 4:11–13. A relationship with Christ has to be the priority, not becoming gifted with the spiritual gifts that should always draw a person to Christianity.

We must be very mindful that there may be other people who are new to Christianity and are still struggling with committing to Christ or are on the fence with their beliefs that He is the Messiah and His teachings are needed in order to go to heaven. If we demand deliverance and total submission without instruction, patience, and love, we will lose their hearts to false teachings and rejection.

Many babes in Christ have an extreme hunger and thirst for righteousness and pleasing God. They are ready and willing to learn and listen to the message of the teacher or preacher in order to grow. A babe in Christ is very impressionable and very vulnerable without the Holy Spirit. Satan knows this and is in real pursuit to take back the souls that just proclaimed their faith in Christ. Satan throws old habits, old flames, and old weaknesses their way to try to lure them back into sin and depravity. Truthfully, they aren't ready to receive the Holy Spirit because they are still learning how to seek the Lord by learning how to pray and, more importantly, how to surrender all to Christ.

The Bible tells us this very simple truth, which is "whoever calls on the name of the Lord shall be saved" (Joel 2:32; NKJV). Therefore, we must start at the basics with new Christians, and that is teaching them the message of Romans 10:9–10 as it reads, "if you confess with your mouth the Lord Jesus and believe in your heart that God has raised Him from the dead, you will be saved. For with the heart one believes unto righteousness, and with the mouth confession is made unto salvation."

The scripture of confession and belief is paramount to salvation or being saved because it surrenders the natural aspects of our minds and body to the authority of the Holy Spirit, and the confession with our hearts reiterates the fact that we are sinful and shameful and need and want a better life. In our hearts, we are inherently sinners coming into the knowledge of Christ; we want to be corrected and delivered. Christ is *that* only answer because we were told in John 3:16 "that whoever believes in Him should not perish but have everlasting life" (NKJV).

The gift of the Holy Spirit are evidence that you are ready to actively work and be effective in establishing the kingdom of God on earth as it is in heaven. Think about it for a moment: What would you envision the kingdom of God to be like? We're not talking about "heaven"; we are talking about the characteristics of the kingdom of the Creator, His attributes, and His presence. Heaven is described in the Bible with physical detail and characteristics of "home." We see this when we read the following scriptures:

- "In My Father's house are many mansions; if *it were* not so, I would have told you. I go to prepare a place for you" (John 14:2; NKJV).
- "Also in front of the throne there was what looked like a sea of glass, clear as crystal. In the center, around the throne, were four living creatures, and they were covered with eyes, in front and in back" (Revelation 4:6; NIV).
- "And he showed me a pure river of water of life, clear as crystal, proceeding from the throne of God and of the Lamb. In

the middle of its street, and on either side of the river, *was* the tree of life, which bore twelve fruits, each *tree* yielding its fruit every month. The leaves of the tree *were* for the healing of the nations. And there shall be no more curse, but the throne of God and of the Lamb shall be in it, and His servants shall serve Him. They shall see His face, and His name *shall be* on their foreheads. There shall be no night there: They need no lamp nor light of the sun, for the Lord God gives them light. And they shall reign forever and ever" (Revelation 22:1–5; NKJV).

The Kingdom of God is so much more. It is the state of the heart and mind of the believer. We must embrace the attributes of Christ and live a life that is faithful to the renewing power of the Holy Spirit, who gives us the fruits and gifts of the spirit of God in Christ, so that there is irrefutable evidence that we have been "born again" into the spirit of holiness and righteousness of God (John 3:5–7).

It's my belief that the process to salvation and being saved is clear:

1. Repent and confess that you are a sinner against God. (Romans 10:9-13)

2. Believe and accept Christ as your personal atonement and Savior for your sinful ways (Romans 10:9–10).

3. Reveal to your concentric circles that you have decided to live a different life than what they have seen you live in the past by submitting to water baptism of repentance and for the forgiveness of sins (Mark 1:4).

4. Strive with your entire heart and mind to build a personal relationship with Christ through prayer, fasting, reading and

studying the Bible, and understanding the life of Christ and who God is (Isaiah 53:4–9; John 1:1–5).

5. Surround yourself with people who understand and desire to be your support and encouragement in this personal and individual process (Romans 14).

6. Put your trust in God first, believe that Christ is always with you, and listen to the Holy Spirit inside of you for clarity, discernment, and instruction on all matters (Proverb 3:5–6; Romans 10:11–17).

7. Open your heart and mind to receiving the Gifts of the Spirit (1 Corinthians 12) by living and functioning with the Fruits of the Spirit (Galatians 5:22–23) in your daily life.

8. Understand why Holy Communion is necessary. (1 Corinthians 11)

CHAPTER FOURTEEN

Can You Believe?

"Jesus said to him, 'If you can believe, all things *are* possible to him who believes.' Immediately the father of the child cried out and said with tears, 'Lord, I believe; help my unbelief!'" (Mark 9:23–24; NKJV)

After all that you have read, can you believe? Now that you've journeyed to the last chapter of this book, I would like to pose a question to you personally and deeply within your heart: Do you believe that God is our Creator, Jesus is the Son of God, and the Holy Spirit comforts and connects us to God by faith through grace? You may be telling yourself, "Well, the facts are interesting, but I'm not sure." Or you might be thinking, "The information I read didn't really clarify some of my questions; besides, there are so many religions and beliefs out there, how can I be sure?" Lastly, you could even reason that "Christianity isn't a faith for everyone; it's just for Jewish people or people of Jewish descent. I'm not Jewish but of another race, so my religion tells me differently."

Throughout the pages of this book, I've tried to introduce a platform that provokes conversation of who the true living God is, meaning many religions believe that there are many gods that played an intricate part in building our earth. There are Roman, Greek, Norse, Egyptian, and, lastly, Buddhist gods, all of which are believed throughout their cultural history and functions to coexist in balance in order to provide mankind with viable spiritual and mental guidance so that they can fully function with peace, grace, obedience, and resolution. Mankind has been divided in its worship and service since mankind's disobedient fall from God's grace.

A. W. Tozer stated in his book *The Knowledge of the Holy*" that "The history of mankind will probably show that no people has ever risen above its religion, a man's spiritual history will positively demonstrate that no religion has ever been greater than its idea of God." [4] Often our idea of God either draws or drives us away from believing that there's an omnipresence that requires our worship. My understanding of what it means *to believe* is when a person has a conviction based on verbal summations that something is true or reliable; it is often used toward a person to suggest a positive outcome in their mental and emotional behavioral process.

To believe allows a person to expand their natural abilities so that the supernatural or highly unattainable can become a part of their reality. When a person believes, they are expressing that they are willing to trust and have faith that a better or greater outcome can and will happen. Additionally, when a person believes, it isn't always positive in nature; sometimes a person may believe negatively in a situation that may cause someone or something else to lose value or importance. That's why it is important to believe that there is a Creator of mankind and that He desires to love each of us and expects us to truly and wholeheartedly love Him back. God the Creator has already expressed to everyone that "He loves us with an everlasting love" and that if we call out to Him, He will hear us and deliver us from any situation or circumstance that is not sanctioned by His purpose and plan.

That's why it is imperative that we believe God loves us individually and His love truly surrounds us every day; when we open our eyes to see a new day and smile and appreciate life, this is God's way of revealing to us His love and mercy for us. He is allowing each of us a chance to believe and have faith in Him for our lives. He is giving us grace and understanding to utilize our freewill to choose Him as the one true God. He desires that we believe, no matter what other belief structures and religions may claim. He wants every individual to personally seek Him as the only way to peace, joy, and happiness, respectfully, while having the faith in believing that there are divine blessings in obedience.

The *Strong's Concordance* 4100 reference and Greek lexical transliteration of the word *believe* (Pisteuo') πιστεύω means, "I believe, Have Faith In, Trust in, I am entrusted with." Therefore, this validates Tozer's statement discussed earlier in the chapter, that mankind needs more than the institutional establishment of religion to feel whole and valued; every person must have a foundation of faith, trust, and belief in a higher calling, a higher being, and a higher purpose. We cannot allow ourselves to not believe that we have a larger destiny and purpose in life.

God plainly outlined in Jeremiah 29:10–13 (NASB) as He was speaking to the Israelites while they were in captivity by the Babylonians and being placated by false prophets and teachers. The false teachers and prophets were trying to assure them that while they were with them, they would have greater riches, peace, and understanding when they conformed to their customs and religions. They wanted the Israelites to believe in what they believed without showing the blessings beforehand. Consequently, God wanted Jeremiah to let His chosen people know that regardless of what their present and future predicaments may be, He is their future, their blessing, and their mercy; all they would have to do was give their hearts and lives to Him in obedience and worship. His words to them were:

> "For thus says the Lord, When seventy years have been completed for Babylon, I will visit you and fulfill My good

word to you, to bring you back to this place. "For I know the plans that I have for you," declares the Lord, "plans for welfare and not for calamity to give you a future and a hope. Then you will call upon Me and come and pray to Me, and I will listen to you. You will seek Me and find *Me* when you search for Me with all your heart." (Jeremiah 29:10–13; NASB)

Today, we must believe that there is purpose and provision for us on the earth. Additionally, we must believe with all our hearts and have faith that something other than ourselves controls our destiny; and if we spiritually connect to God, who is our Creator and life source, then we will be able to overcome any situation that we may encounter. That's why it is important to seek God and trust that He loves us so much He has already carved out our lives to be blessed and filled with purpose and meaning. This has been stated thousands of years prior to me writing this today. Consequentially, it was written over 2,000 years ago, that God so love the world that He allowed His son to become a willing sacrifice for our atonement; so that whoever, regardless of your religion, race, social status, or physical attributes; can sincerely, believe in God's mercy through his son Jesus; they will feel God's grace through faith and know that they are now saved and shielded by the love of God through faith.

The words *faith* and *believe* are often interchangeable in their understanding as we begin to describe how we feel and think about God. In the Bible's Old Testament scriptures, faith carries multiple meanings relating to trusting in God. This is also relational to understanding that trusting in God also means that you are acting in obedience to His divine purpose and plan for your life; faith in the Old Testament is also outlined in many passages of clarity that God is the Creator, the Sustainer of life, and the Controller of history (Psalm 19:24). Also, there are examples of how people in the Ancient Near East (ANE) and biblical scriptures believed in the one true God around 3,500 years ago. The people of Nineveh, the great pagan capital of Assyria, "believed in God" when Jonah the prophet came to warn them of impending destruction, and as a result, they began fasting, praying, and repenting for God's mercy (Jonah 3:4–5; NASB).

Another example is written in the Bible how Abraham believed God and "it accounted him to righteousness" (Gen 15:6 NKJV). Lastly, in the New Testament, the apostle Paul confirms that the true value of a Christian is his understanding and ability to fully believe that God raised Christ from the dead (Roman 10:9–10). God wants us to become Disciples of Christ and fully believe in Him so that we can effectively take the message of salvation faithfully and without fear to others who may be like the Ninevites or the Israelites, who seem to be destined for destruction due to their disobedience and sinful ways.

Faith is the catalyst by which God's power is made visible, meaning faith moves spiritual and emotional mountains, faith heals the sick, but more importantly, faith is the means of entrance into the kingdom of heaven. Where is your faith? Do you believe that Jesus is the Son of God? Can you believe that all things are possible when you believe? Has there been a miraculous situation in your life that you believe only God was able to do it? Chances are it was God revealing His presence in your circumstance and in your life so that you could see the goodness of God working in your life. Can you think of any other times that you were at your limit emotionally or socially where you were faced with something you had no idea of how you would be able to survive or overcome? But you remembered to say these words, "Oh my God," "God, help me," and "Please, God." This is the pronouncement of God being called into your situation; to confirm this, we find that in the Bible passage of Jeremiah 33:3 NKJV how God said, "Call to Me, and I will answer you, and show you great and mighty things, which you do not know."

God wants a relationship with you and wants you to call out to Him when you are hurting or can't see any other alternative. He wants to reveal His love and strength in your life just as He revealed Himself in so many others. God desires us to live a life of righteousness and faith so that we can be called men and women of God who are considered righteous in God's eyes to bear witness to the truth. Paul writes in Romans 3:21–22 (NASB), "But now apart from the Law *the* righteousness of God has been manifested, being witnessed by the Law and the Prophets, even *the* righteousness of God through faith in Jesus Christ for all those who believe; for there is no distinction." This means that the principles of the Old Testament call to obedience unto the laws and commandments can be revealed through our faith and believe in Jesus Christ as Messiah and Savior. His death, burial, and resurrection essentially tore the Old Testament veil that shielded the "Holy of Holies" (Hebrews 9:1–9; NASB) and the establishment of the new covenant by faith through grace and His ultimate sacrifice (Hebrews 9:10–16).

That is why it is important to internalize the magnitude of how God loves His creation (us) so much that He provided us with a way to be redeemed from the sinful nature of Adam and Eve's collaboration with Satan to undermine the will of God in order to introduce the freewill of sin to all mankind linked through an inherited bloodline of disobedience to God. I remember my grandmother illustrating to me how the conversation with the triune may have been just before God spoke into existence life. She told me, "God said, 'Let us make man,'" and the Holy Spirit stated, "But if we make man, man will sin." Then, Jesus said, "If they sin, then I will redeem them."

Since the creation of time, God has always wanted a relationship with us; He has always desired to rekindle the walks in the garden just like He had with Adam in the Garden of Eden. God wants to walk with you and speak to you in a whisper just like He spoke with Elijah during his time of distress and need. That is why He sent the

Holy Spirit to lead us and guide us as we continue to build a lasting relationship with God; the Holy Spirit is our teacher and comforter when times are so unbearable and we are unsure of our purpose. He allows us to hear God's voice as a whisper to soothe our hearts when we are sick or depressed with life. He helps us to understand God's message of obedience and trust so that we won't sin against Him. The Son is our intercessor when we have sinned or fallen short of God's glory. The Son is our advocate when the accuser of the brethren stands before God to give account of our sins and shames. The Son, Jesus Christ, is the Great Physician when we are sick or when the evils of illness or infirmity strike our bodies. Jesus Christ is the way, the truth, and the life; when we have given up on life and believe that all hope is lost. He is the way to acceptance of God's love, mercy, and grace in confession that He is Lord, He is one with God, He is the Word with God, and the Word was God.

When we come to believe that all things are possible, shouldn't we also believe that God created the heavens and the earth, the Holy Spirit fills and comfort those that willingly receive Him into their hearts, and, without a doubt, Jesus Christ is the Son of God who came from heaven as fully man and fully God to redeem each of us from our past, present, and future selves, from sin? He healed the lame man at a pool called Bethesda, He fixed a man's withered hand, He made a man's blindness correct itself, He exorcized a legion of demons from a man, He raised the dead, and He will save and give you a new and fresh outlook on life. All you have to do is believe, trust, and acknowledge that you have sinned against God and no longer desire to live a life that displeases Him. Accept Jesus's gift of salvation by deeply internalizing Romans 10:9–17 (NASB) as it reads:

> "If you confess with your mouth Jesus *as* Lord, and believe
> in your heart that God raised Him from the dead, you will
> be saved; for with the heart a person believes, resulting in

righteousness, and with the mouth he confesses, resulting in salvation. For the Scripture says, "Whoever believes in Him will not be disappointed." For there is no distinction between Jew and Greek; for the same *Lord* is Lord of all, abounding in riches for all who call on Him; for "Whoever will call on the name of the Lord will be saved." How then will they call on Him in whom they have not believed? How will they believe in Him whom they have not heard? And how will they hear without a preacher? How will they preach unless they are sent? Just as it is written, "How beautiful are the feet of those who bring good news of good things!" However, they did not all heed the good news; for Isaiah says, "Lord, who has believed our report?" So, faith *comes* from hearing, and hearing by the word of Christ."

FINAL THOUGHTS

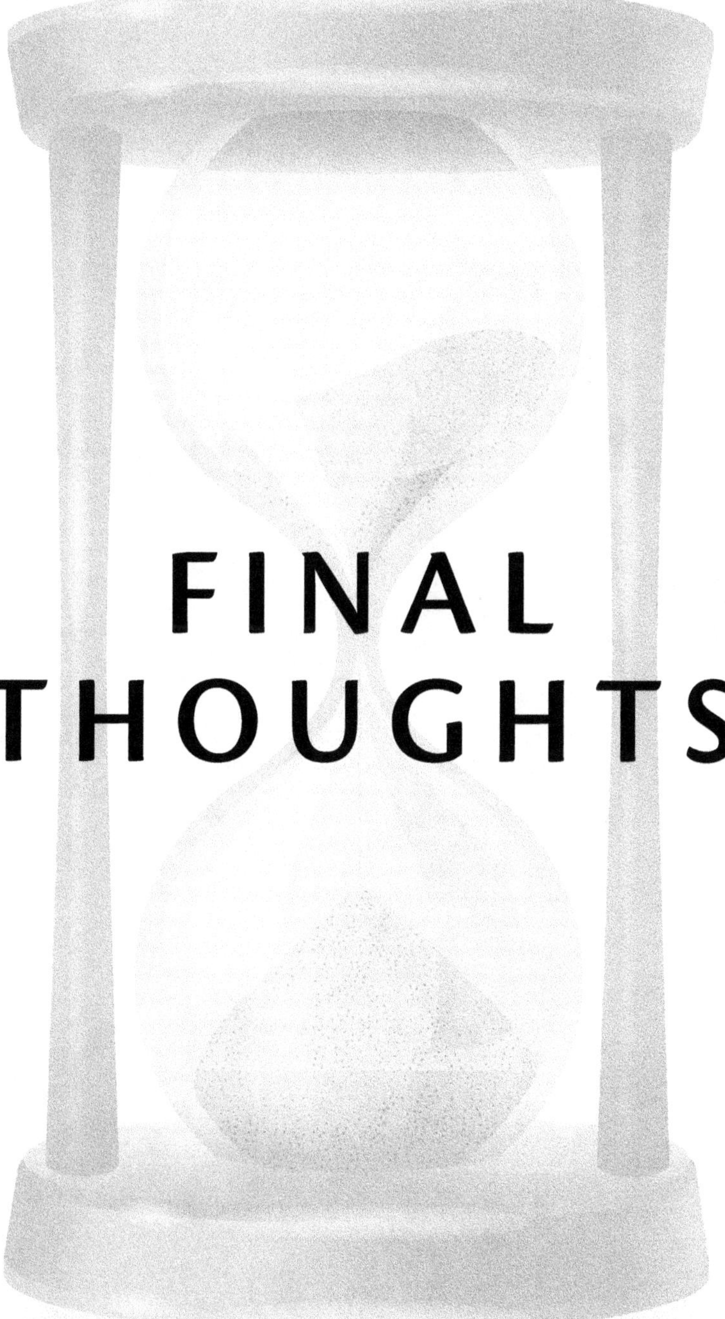

Final Thoughts

"The grace of the Lord Jesus Christ, and the love of God, and the communion of the Holy Spirit *be* with you all. Amen." 2 Corinthians 13:14 NKJV

The scripture written above has been a staple of closing service or worship in some churches worldwide. They call it "The Benediction." However, if we really take the time to read and understand the composition, we will realize just how profound this brief yet mighty statement has just charged the atmosphere. In the Old Testament, grace was revealed by God when God told Abram to leave his severely infested town filled with pagan worship and mysticism to become the father of Judaism and of God's chosen, the Jewish people.

There was unmerited favor that God had toward Abraham (Abram's name changed to Abraham) when He told him that he would be a great nation and the father of many nations because of Abraham's unmerited propensity to believe that there is only one true God.

Additionally, grace was shown to Hananiah, Mishael, and Azariah (also known as the three Hebrew boys Shadrach, Meshach, and Abednego) when they were condemned to what was meant to be a fiery death by King Nebuchadnezzar, but the unmerited favor of God sat in the midst of the fire and rested, ruled, and abided with them.

Now is the time to believe that tomorrow is not promised and decide where you will spend eternity. Will you spend it with God, worshipping and praising Him for His grace and mercy, or will you be cast into the darkness prepared for the devil, his angels, and all unbelievers? Please accept Christ today as your personal Savior; He has a mansion and all the provisions that you will ever need on earth and in heaven. It takes a leap of faith and trust right here, right now to be sealed by the power of the blood of Christ. You won't be condemned by God, and you surely will not be turned away from Jesus for your decision. They love you enough to promise you that They will be with you every step of the way.

Now is the time to believe that Christ is the only way to heaven and God is the Almighty God of all creation. Don't you see? Jesus is returning to establish the kingdom of God on earth, but we must be saved and sealed with the gift of the Holy Spirit in order to be counted as redeemed. Every day, someone, unfortunately, dies without accepting Christ as their Savior. Many of them either didn't believe or thought they had more time. What if you died today? Can you say that you've accepted Christ as your personal Savior and are counted as redeemed and sanctified? That's why accepting salvation is an individual and relational endeavor because tomorrow isn't promised to anyone and the choice to accept Him is NOW!

Paul wanted us to know that Jesus has the power to defeat sin and death. He has the power to defeat all spiritual bondages in your life. He is the beginning and the end. He is the Great Physician. He is the Son of God. 2 Timothy 1:9–10 (NKJV) tells us that God is the One

who has saved us and called *us* with a holy calling, not according to our works, but according to His own purpose and grace which was given to us in Christ Jesus before time began, but has now been revealed by the appearing of our Savior Jesus Christ, *who* has abolished death and brought life and immortality to light through the gospel.

Jesus already understood what God revealed in the book of Joel that, in the "last days," His Spirit will be poured out on all nations. The Spirit of the Lord is still on the earth, and He is waiting for your answer to the call on your lives to allow your hearts and souls to be filled and sealed with the Holy Spirit. However, Satan has everyone duped into believing that there is no heaven or hell and that works and practices of traditional and ritualistic feasts and ordinances is enough to please God. Satan wants us to believe that there are "understood facts" about God, salvation, and redemption that are considered to be the right ways to understand the knowledge of God or the Spirit of God. Satan wants us to believe that keeping traditions, rituals, sacrificial feasts, and festivals will allow us to attain eternal life when those same festivals and feasts weren't enough to allow the children of Israel to enter the Promised Land. That's why a total redirection and a spiritual renewal has to take place in our hearts and minds in order to transform our hearts and minds back to seeking God in Christ for the way, the truth, and the life. This calls for a prayerful request to God to "renew the right spirit within us."

Satan wants us to believe that all is well because he has allowed the god mammon to roam this earth freely, distributing the prospects of riches, indulgences, and self-willed prideful thinking. He is the deceiver and the great liar. You cannot trust the mind and spirit that rest within you to believe that "when we die, there's nothing, or it will be a reunion with family and old friends" because your unrepentant mind was shaped in sin and inheritably sinful. Our televisions are always depicting demonic suggestions and satanic ideologies to desensitize everyone to the impending destruction. This can be seen as we notice that some of the highest and most popularly watched television shows or movies have characters who deal with witchcraft, idolatry, monsters, aliens, devils, demons, wolves, vampires, and, of course, zombies.

Society has embraced death, lewdness, and unnatural prefer-
ences because the charms of the "prince of the air" (Ephesians 2:2; 2
Corinthians 4:4) still rule the land that we live in. Violence, death,
and blatant disrespect for others' rights to live, move, and have their
existence has grown exponentially in everyday life. People are more
willing to kill or be killed instead of learning how to be a peacemaker
or forgiver of those who "trespass against them." Sexual promiscuity
and immorality are no longer a "closet thing"; instead, they have
become the focal point of society, regardless of the fact that sexual
immorality has severely damaged homes, relationships, and families.

We must get to the core reason why people believe that sin should
be a normal way of life. The core reason is to destroy and kill the
generational advancements of the bloodlines of the participants in
hopes to deny the birthing of a person who will be a great addition and
asset to their communities and to God's plan for mankind. Healing,
deliverance, and forgiveness are needed to heal the generations who
believe that everything should be acceptable and embraced so that a
person's freewill can remain intact. There is a way to restore peace,
balance, and joy back into the lives of families that have been separated
or destroyed by the influences of Satan. 2 Chronicles 7:14 (NKJV)
supports restoration and forgiveness when we are given the answer
by God that "if My people who are called by My name will humble
themselves, and pray and seek My face, and turn from their wicked
ways, then I will hear from heaven, and will forgive their sin and
heal their land."

The chains and influences of Satan must be broken before you
die. The desire and acceptance of depravity must be released in order
to accept salvation before you die. You must be born again—not of
body but of spirit. You can't make that decision on your own because
the thing that you are fighting is spiritual wickedness in high places.
You are in the fight of your life against the principalities of evil. That's
why it is important to believe that there is and will be a place where

there will be no more crying and fighting against evil and hatred. The Bible tells us that death and hell will be destroyed (Revelation 20:14) in the second death.

Again, spiritual salvation is offered to you today. Now is the time to believe that you are special and greater than your situation. You have an intercessor that is in constant adjudication for your spiritual life. He wants us to desire not a life in Him that "looks good" but a life that will "be good" because we have been set apart through the cleansing of our hearts and minds through the Holy Spirit.

It's 2016, and there is so much killing and violence in the earth; Jesus told us that the last days would consist of these things and that we should start to take heed and not get complacent. The Bible, which was written hundreds of years before this time, is filled with prophecies that outline the behavior and coming violence and moral detachment that mankind will start to embrace (Matthew 24:11–12; 2 Timothy 3:2–4; Philippians 3:18–19; 1 Timothy 4:1–2; 2 Timothy 4:3–4).

Every day, someone's time is up in this life and eternity has begun for them. We have to wonder if that person heeded to the call of salvation and accepted God as Creator and Christ as their Savior. It's important to understand that we only have this time on earth, this time in between the born and death dates to believe. Our life span is the moment to believe; tomorrow is not promised, and the decision of "I believe" or "I don't believe" is pressed daily before us and in our hearts every day that we wake up and enjoy life. The Bible clearly gives an understanding that time is precious and the time that we have to listen, accept, and worship God is very limited. Hebrews 9:27(NKJV) tells us, "And as it is appointed for men to die once, but after this the judgment." After you die, it's too late. Now is the time to believe, accept Christ as your Savior, and turn from the influences of sin and evil.

Jesus left us with instructions to "go," offer salvation to those that are not in fellowship with Christ, and ask them a simple question:

"Will you accept Christ as your personal Savior?" He also wanted us to be willing to love people where they are spiritually and emotionally, meaning to go to them and tell them to have faith in God and allow Him to govern their lives so that peace and joy can finally be attained. Also, those that are hurting and have been abused, ignored, mistreated, and emotionally hurt so badly, until they no longer believe that God cares and are reachable. Now is the time to believe that God was there all the time, protecting you from a more painful or harmful attack from Satan and the influences of this earth that could have totally destroyed you. However, you were saved and spared another chance to be a testimony of strength, courage, and love to someone that is completely bound in hatred, loneliness, and living behind the mask of shame and low self-esteem.

Now is the time to believe that there is hope, health, and healing; but, we must first wholeheartedly believe that all things are possible with Christ and we know that He heals, delivers, and restores.

Salvation Prayer

God, I am sorry for not taking You seriously in my life in the past. I'm sorry that I've ignored the love and mercy that You have shown me each day. I ask You to forgive me of all the sins that I have committed. Forgive me of all the known and unknown sins that I have committed. I acknowledge that I am a sinner, and I am sorry for my sins and the life that I have lived. I need Your forgiveness, and I also need to forgive those that have hurt, abused, and cursed my life. I believe that Your only begotten Son, Jesus Christ, died for my sins on the cross at Calvary, and I am now willing to turn from my sins. I accept the gift of salvation that You extended to me when You gave Your only Son, Jesus, as a voluntary sacrifice.

You spoke to me through your Holy Word in Romans 10:9 that if I confess the Lord our God and believe in my heart that God raised Jesus from the dead, then I shall be saved. Right now, with all my heart and mind, I confess Jesus as the Lord of my soul. With my heart, I believe that God raised Jesus from the dead. I accept Jesus Christ as my own personal Savior, and according to His Word, I am saved.

Thank You, Jesus, for Your love and grace which have saved me, by faith, from my sins. I thank You, Jesus, that Your grace seals me to You. I thank You for giving me strength to forgive and release my heart from the grips of pain, sin, and shame. Transform my life so that I may bring glory and honor only to You and not to myself. Thank You, Jesus, for eternal life.

This I pray in Jesus name,
Amen

Scriptures to Understand Salvation

John 3:16 (NKJV) For God so loved the world that He gave His only begotten Son, that whoever believes in Him should not perish but have everlasting life.

Romans 6:23 (NKJV) For the wages of sin *is* death, but the gift of God *is* eternal life in Christ Jesus our Lord.

Romans 3:23 (NKJV) for all have sinned and fall short of the glory of God,

Romans 5:8 (NKJV) But God demonstrates His own love toward us, in that while we were still sinners, Christ died for us.

Psalm 103:12 (NKJV) As far as the east is from the west, *So* far has He removed our transgressions from us.

Acts 4:12 (NKJV) Nor is there salvation in any other, for there is no other name under heaven given among men by which we must be saved."

1 Peter 3:18 (NKJV) For Christ also suffered once for sins, the just for the unjust, that He might bring us to God, being put to death in the flesh but made alive by the Spirit,

1 John 1:9 (NKJV) If we confess our sins, He is faithful and just to forgive us *our* sins and to cleanse us from all unrighteousness.

Mark 1:15 (NKJV) and saying, "The time is fulfilled, and the kingdom of God is at hand. Repent, and believe in the gospel."

John 3:17 (NKJV) For God did not send His Son into the world to condemn the world, but that the world through Him might be saved

Revelation 3:20 (NKJV) Behold, I stand at the door and knock. If anyone hears My voice and opens the door, I will come in to him and dine with him, and he with Me.

John 10:9 (NKJV) I am the door. If anyone enters by Me, he will be saved, and will go in and out and find pasture.

Mark 16:16 (NKJV) He who believes and is baptized will be saved; but he who does not believe will be condemned.

Romans 6:4 (NKJV) Therefore we were buried with Him through baptism into death, that just as Christ was raised from the dead by the glory of the Father, even so we also should walk in newness of life.

2 Corinthians 5:17 (NKJV) Therefore, if anyone *is* in Christ, *he is* a new creation; old things have passed away; behold, all things have become new

Romans 10:13 (NKJV) For "whoever calls on the name of the Lord shall be saved."

Romans 10:9-10 (NKJV) that if you confess with your mouth the Lord Jesus and believe in your heart that God has raised Him from the dead, you will be saved. For with the heart one believes unto righteousness, and with the mouth confession is made unto salvation.

Acts 15:11 (NKJV) But we believe that through the grace of the Lord Jesus Christ we shall be saved in the same manner as they."

Ephesians 2:8-9 (NKJV) For by grace you have been saved through faith, and that not of yourselves; *it is* the gift of God, not of works, lest anyone should boast.

Titus 3:5 (NKJV) not by works of righteousness which we have done, but according to His mercy He saved us, through the washing of regeneration and renewing of the Holy Spirit,

1 John 5:11-13 (NKJV) And this is the testimony: that God has given us eternal life, and this life is in His Son. He who has the Son has life; he who does not have the Son of God does not have life. These things I have written to you who believe in the name of the Son of God, that you may know that you have eternal life, and that you may *continue to* believe in the name of the Son of God.

John 8:36 (NKJV) Therefore if the Son makes you free, you shall be free indeed.

Luke 8:12 (NKJV) Those by the wayside are the ones who hear; then the devil comes and takes away the word out of their hearts, lest they should believe and be saved.

Matthew 24:13 (NKJV) But he who endures to the end shall be saved.

Acts 16:31 (NKJV) So they said, "Believe on the Lord Jesus Christ, and you will be saved, you and your household."

1 John 4:19 (NKJV) We love Him because He first loved us.

Luke 7:50 (NKJV) Then He said to the woman, "Your faith has saved you. Go in peace."

Acts 2:47 (NKJV) praising God and having favor with all the people. And the Lord added to the church daily those who were being saved.

Romans 10:9-10 (NKJV) that if you confess with your mouth the Lord Jesus and believe in your heart that God has raised Him from the dead, you will be saved. For with the heart one believes unto righteousness, and with the mouth confession is made unto salvation.

About the Author - Thomas E. Walker

The history of Thomas's commitment to his Christian faith started in 1976, when he first accepted Jesus Christ as Lord and Savior. He was baptized in Lake Michigan on a warm sunrise Sunday morning, while serving under the Leadership Elder Jefferson and William Campbell and the Church of God In Christ teachings at Amazing Church of God In Christ. Thomas served as a Jr. Deacon from the age of 10 – 16 years old. He was a choir member, organist, taught and participated heavily in Sunday School, Young People Willing Workers (Y.P.W.W.), Bible Band, Home and Foreign Mission.

In 1983, Thomas joined First Corinthians M.B. Church in Chicago, IL under the leadership and strong biblical teachings of Rev. Harvey Spivey where he actively served as a tenor in the Voices of Victory choir under the inspiring teachings of Evangelist Angela Spivey. She inspired him to believe that singing for the Lord was the greatest way to give thanks when you are living a life that honors Him. So, Thomas continued to sing in the choir until he enlisted in the U.S. ARMY in 1985 where he served until retirement at the rank of Sergeant in 2003. Additionally, in 1993 Thomas served as Regional Coordinator for the Illinois National Guard's Challenge Program where he helped at risk teens ages 16-18 years old to complete their GED within a structured quasi-military environment. In 2005, Thomas attended DeVry University, where he obtained a Bachelors of Science degree of Technical Management with a concentration in Small Business

Entrepreneurship. After graduating, he started his own business called Walkus Consulting Solutions in Plainfield, IL in the Spring of 2008.

In 2008, Thomas was blessed to serve under the leadership of Pastor D.D. Nabor, of the Covenant of Faith Community Church where he was a member of the Praise Team Ministries. Later that year, and after more than 16 years; Thomas answered the call to ministry and began a life of re-dedication, restoration, and complete devotion to the Word of God. In 2010, he served as assistant pastor, intercessory prayer team and performed ministerial duties at Glory Rock World Ministries.

In 2010, God ordered his steps to Bolingbrook Community Church in Bolingbrook, IL; where Pastor Calvin Quarles teaching and advisement to serve and evangelize; impacted him to reach those who were looking for hope and teach them how to "Let go and Let God." Christ further appointed and instructed him and his wife, Evangelist Denise P. Ford-Walker; in 2010, to begin their Evangelistic outreach ministry called Reflections of Grace Outreach Ministries where they are currently founders and ministers in Moreno Valley, California. In 2014, Thomas Graduated from Liberty Theological Seminary with his Masters in Christian Ministry and special interest in Pastoral Counseling. Now (2016), He is completing his Masters of Divinity in Pastoral Counseling at Liberty School of Divinity. Thomas E. Walker has a blended family of six children and six grandchildren; he resides in Moreno Valley, California.

Thomas authored a non-fiction book of inspiration about his life's testimony and faith entitled *"My Steps Have Already Been Ordered; what happens when free will is not free."*

Favorite Books

1. Anderson, N. T. *The Bondage Breaker.* Eugene: Harvest House, 2000.

2. Blomberg, Craig, L.; Markley, Jennifer F. *A Handbook of New Testament Exgesis.* Grand Rapids: Baker Academic, 2010.

3. Boa, Kenneth. *Conformed to His Image: Biblical and Practical Approaches to Spiritual Formation.* Grand Rapids: Zondervan, 2001.

4. DeRouchie, J. *What the Old Testament Authors Really Cared About: A Survey of Jesus' Bible.* Grand Rapids: Kregel Academic, 2013.

5. Enns, P. *The Moody Handbook of Theology, Revised and Expanded.* Chicago: Moody Publishers, 2008.

6. Fay, William, and Linda Evans Shepherd. *Share Jesus without Fear.* Nashville: B&H, 1999.

7. Ferguson, E. *Church History Volume One: From Christ to Pre-Reformation.* Grand Rapids: Zondervan, 2005.

8. Ford, D. P. *Praying to Know Him: Praying From My Soul.* Atlanta: Walkus Consulting Solutions, 2014.

9. Grudem, W. *Systematic Theology.* Grand Rapids: Zondervan, 2000.

10. Horton, D. *The Portable Seminary: A Master's Level Overview in One Volume*. Grand Rapids: Baker, 2006.

11. Hyatt, E. *2000 Years of Christianity: A 21st Century Look at Church History from a Pentecostal Charismatic Perspective*. FL: Charisma House, 2002.

12. James, K. (n.d.). *Holy Bible*.

13. Köstenberger, Andreas J., L. Scott Kellum, and Charles L. Quarles. *The Cradle, the Cross, and the Crown: An Introduction to the New Testament*. Nashville: B&H Publishing, 2009.

14. Merrill, Eugene H., Mark F. Booker, and Michael A Cristanti. *The World and the Word: An Introduction to the Old Testament*. Nashville: B&H Publishing, 2011.

15. Nellum-Jones, A. *Poems of My Imprisionment*. Detroit: Walkus Consulting Solutions, 2010.

16. Smith, Felicia. *Seeds of Hope*. USA: Queen Dream Publishing, 2014.

17. Townsel, M. D. *Ten Moments of Healing*. Apopka: Certa, 2013.

18. Walker, T. E. *My Steps Have Already Been Ordered: What Happens When Freewill Is Not Free*. Chicago: Walkus Consulting Solutions, 2008.

19. Walton, J. H. *Ancient Near Eastern Thought and the Old Testament: Introducing the Conceptual World of the Hebrew Bible*. Grand Rapids: Baker Academics, 2006.

20. Warren, J. *A Letter to the Angels: A Guide for the Future Direction of the Church.* USA: Kingdom Scribes Publishing, 2007.

21. Whitney, Donald S. *Spiritual Disciplines for the Christian Life.* Colorado Springs: NAVPRESS, 2014.

22. Wilson, S. D. *Hurt People Hurt People: Hope and Healing for Yourself and Your Relationships.* Grand Rapids: Discovery House, 2011.

Bibliography

1. Friberg, Timothy, Barbara Friberg, and Neva F. Miller. *Analytical Lexicon of the Greek New Testament*. Victoria: Trafford Publishing, 2005.

2. Blomberg, Craig, L. ; Markley, Jennifer F. *A Handbook of New Testament Exgesis*. Grand Rapids: Baker Academic, 2010.

3. Strong, J. *Enhanced Strong's Lexicon*. Woodside: Woodside Bible Fellowship, 1995.

4. Tozer, A. W. *The Knowledge of the Holy*. New York: Harper Collins, 1978.

5. Lockman Foundation. (1995). *Bible, New American Standard NASB95*. CA: NASB95.

6. Merriam-Webster. *Merriam-Webster's Collegiate Dictionary*. Merriam-Webster, Inc, 2012.

www.ingramcontent.com/pod-product-compliance
Lightning Source LLC
Chambersburg PA
CBHW050116280326
41933CB00010B/1119